Pr

Understanding

MW00416623

"Cory Jensen provides a scripturally rich exploration of the symbols, covenants, and experiences the temple uses to instruct and inspire us. I love his focus on deepening our covenant relationship with God, whose presence we seek. If you're looking for motivation to attend the temple more often, or gain greater insight into its transformative potential, you'll find plenty of both in these pages."

—Wendy Ulrich, PhD, author of
The Temple Experience: Our Journey Toward Holiness

"You have to read this book. Your knowledge and understanding of the temple will never be the same afterward."

—Lisa Roylance

"Cory Jensen has written a thoughtful and beautiful discourse on a vital and sensitive subject—the temple endowment. Most young people go to the temple for the first time unprepared. Jensen unravels the mystery and shares insights with the reader that answer the most important question of all: why? I highly recommend it."

—Mark L. Petersen, CEO of Mentors International,
author of *He Chose Life: Nathan's Story*

"I found everything contained within *Understanding Your Endowment* completely appropriate to discuss and presented gospel truths simply and clearly. This is a straightforward presentation that is soundly based upon the scriptures and Latter-day General Authorities that will help us all be better prepared to attend the temple again and again to be taught from on high."

—David Whitlock, former LDS bishop

"I can truthfully see one person being trained to teach this book in every ward. This book is long overdue."

—Larry Covington, ordinance worker
at the Mount Timpanogos Temple

Mentors International

Mentors International is all about helping to lift the poor to become self-reliant. They do this by helping aspiring entrepreneurs—most of them being women who are trying to support their children—receive critical business training, make small loans, and get work with dignity to support their families. Mentors provides a hand-*up* rather than a hand*out*.

As these loans are repaid, the funds are redeployed to help other families in need. In this way, donations to Mentors become perpetual gifts.

Over the past twenty-five years, Mentors has helped lift over 3.5 million individuals and their families out of poverty and onto the path to prosperity. For further information, or to make a donation, visit www.mentorsinternational.org. All of the author's proceeds from this book are being donated to Mentors and other charitable organizations that serve those in need around the world.

Understanding

❧ YOUR ❧

ENDOWMENT

May God bless you~

[signature]

Understanding
❧ YOUR ❧
ENDOWMENT

CORY B. JENSEN

CFI
An Imprint of Cedar Fort, Inc.
Springville, Utah

ISBN 13: 978-1-4621-1743-7

Published by CFI, an imprint of Cedar Fort, Inc.
2373 W. 700 S., Springville, UT 84663
Distributed by Cedar Fort, Inc., www.cedarfort.com

LIBRARY OF CONGRESS CATALOGING-IN-PUBLICATION DATA

Jensen, Cory B., 1966- author.
Understanding your endowment / Cory B. Jensen.
   pages cm
Discusses how to enrich the temple experience for members of The Church of Jesus Christ of Latter-day Saints by focusing on the ordinances and their purpose.
Includes bibliographical references.
ISBN 978-1-4621-1743-7
1. Temple work (Mormon Church) 2. Temple endowments (Mormon Church) 3. Symbolism--Religious aspects--Church of Jesus Christ of Latter-day Saints. 4. Church of Jesus Christ of Latter-day Saints--Doctrines. 5. Mormon Church--Doctrines. I. Title.
BX8643.T4J46 2015
264'.09332--dc23
                    2015009396

Cover design by Shawnda T. Craig
Cover design © 2015 Lyle Mortimer
Edited and typeset by Kevin Haws

Printed in the United States of America

10 9 8 7 6 5 4 3 2

Printed on acid-free paper

To all who share a love for the temple.

Contents

Acknowledgments

So many people have influenced this work and blessed my life. First and foremost, my eternal sweetheart and companion: Traci. Our lives are so closely intertwined and connected that mine would be pointless without her. Traci, you mean everything to me.

I am also forever indebted to my parents and grandparents: Brent and Jerrilyn Jensen, Vaughn and Marlene Nielson, Mckay and Gwen Loveland, and Dewey and Cloree Jensen. Thank you for your love, your sacrifices in raising me, and your efforts in teaching me the gospel.

I have been blessed with four amazing children and one incredible son-in-law. You have all taught me so much. Jessica, Devin, Jenny, Nathan, and Danny: no father could ask for better children. And Jess, thank you for all your feedback and invaluable help with earlier drafts. You're a great writer.

My understanding of the temple has been greatly influenced by several good friends, including Craig Jenkins. Some of what you have taught me appears within these pages. I also appreciate my great business partners, Daniel Gunnell, Kimball Hodges, and Brad Gunnell, for their suggestions and support. A big thank you to Lauren Larsen,

Acknowledgments

Amanda Smith, Stephanie Nichols, and Matthew Kennedy for the illustrations and photography.

I would also like to publicly acknowledge the many people who have influenced and blessed my life. There are too many to list, but you know who you are. With all my heart, I thank each and every one of you.

A huge thank-you also goes to the helpful staff at Cedar Fort, including Emily Chambers, Shawnda Craig, Kelly Martinez, Kevin Haws, Rebecca Greenwood, and Mary-Celeste Lewis.

Finally, I owe everything to my Jesus (see 2 Nephi 33:6), and humbly dedicate this work to Him. Without Him, our temples would be meaningless. His love, condescension, and grace, offered so freely to all of us, overwhelm me.

Preface

Do you ever feel like there is something more to the temple, but you aren't quite getting it? Perhaps, at times, you have even found yourself distracted or bored in a temple session. It doesn't need to be that way.

Coming to understand our own endowment is a personal, sacred journey, one largely between us individually and the Lord. No one, other than the Lord, is really qualified to unfold everything, and much of that will come quietly through the Spirit. Part of the beauty of the temple's ordinances and teaching lies in the fact that the Lord can personalize them to whatever stage we are at in our individual growth. The path to understanding requires time, effort, and experience. Sometimes it may seem a bit overwhelming. We may need some help, or at least a foundation from which to begin.

The intent of this book is to help lay that foundation and enrich your temple experience. It is written for believing Latter-day Saints who would like to better understand their own temple endowment. President David O. McKay once stated,

> I have met so many young people who have been disappointed after they have gone through the House of the Lord. They have been

honest in that disappointment. Some of them have shed tears as they have opened their hearts and expressed heart-felt sorrow that they did not see and hear and feel what they had hoped to see and hear and feel. I have analyzed those confessions as I have listened to them, and I have come to the conclusion that in nearly every case it was the person's fault. He or she has failed to comprehend the significance of the message that is given in the Temple.[1]

It's not just the youth who feel this way. Many adult members sense deeply the temple's importance but don't feel they understand it all that well.

So where do we turn for help? *Understanding Your Endowment* provides some context and a foundation from the scriptures to assist you in recognizing the meaning of the temple and its purpose in your individual life. It is not intended as a scholarly publication. Nor is it an apologetic work defending the temple. It is not meant to be comprehensive, but it may give you some new ways to view the temple. It is my earnest hope and prayer that it will aid you in coming to understand your own endowment.

If your circumstances permit, I highly recommend you attend the temple weekly. Doing so will change and bless your life in ways you likely won't anticipate. It has certainly done so for me. Being in the temple regularly has by far been one of the greatest blessings of my life; it has blessed my marriage and family and made me a much better person. It has anchored me and helped me through the most difficult years of my life. The Lord has given me peace there, even while storms raged all around.

Over the past thirty years, my understanding of the temple has grown immensely, but I still feel like a slow learner when it comes to these things. I have found myself bored at times and felt like I wasn't getting it at other times. It has taken me many years, much study, and some patient instruction by the Spirit to gain the understanding I possess. Along the way, I've had a few good teachers that have helped tremendously. I am very indebted to them. Even so, things are still unfolding, and I am still learning from the temple. Some people say they learn something new every time they attend. It has not been that way for me, but insights have come line upon line with persistent attendance and effort.

We all need the joy of discovery. We tend to value what we work and struggle for. That which is too easily obtained is often not treasured. Each of us must labor to gain understanding. This book will not attempt to give you all the answers—nor do I believe I possess all of them. This text merely provides a starting point from which to begin. At the end of many of the chapters, you will find suggested "homework" for further study. But even then, recognize that the temple is such a vast topic that we will only scratch the surface here. We all need to seek further learning by study and by faith (see D&C 109:14).

Sometimes, as a people, we are so reticent to speak of the temple that we say almost nothing. Perhaps we need to say a bit more. This work tries to maintain an appropriate balance. President Benson remarked, "Because of its sacredness we are sometimes reluctant to say anything about the temple to our children and grandchildren. As a consequence . . . when they go there, they do so without much background to prepare them for the obligations and covenants they enter into. I believe a proper understanding or background will immeasurably help prepare our youth for the temple."[2]

Some show up at the temple to receive their endowments without a clue as to what to expect. Their initial experience could have greater meaning if they had some background and context with which to better understand it. Like the Ethiopian man taught by Philip, new endowees may need some guidance and help, especially at the beginning (see Acts 8:26–39). At an appropriate time, you may wish to use parts of what is contained herein as a resource to prepare your children or grandchildren for their temple experience. This book actually began as a paper I wrote to help my oldest daughter prepare to receive her endowment.

Our discussion of the temple will be based primarily upon the scriptures. The Lord holds the temple and its ordinances sacred. I hope it is the same for you. There will not be any discussion of elements that we have covenanted not to disclose, and I will seek to approach this topic with deep reverence and humility.[3]

I alone am responsible for the content of this book. It does not in any way represent official doctrine of The Church of Jesus Christ of Latter-day Saints. Though it represents my beliefs, it is by no means exhaustive or error free. I am certain there are things contained herein that ten years from now I may see differently. Take what seems right and helpful to you and please discard anything that doesn't. Part of the genius and beauty of the symbolism in the temple is that it allows the Lord to personalize and customize the experience to our individual needs and circumstances. Your understanding may be different from mine. And that is completely fine.

With that disclaimer, let's begin.

CHAPTER 1

Covenants

Suppose you were teaching a class of Israelite youth in biblical times and posed the question: "What is a covenant?" Would they have responded that a covenant is a two-way promise? Probably not. Ancient Israel didn't claim to be the Lord's "two-way promise" people. They were the Lord's covenant people and understood covenants in terms of a sacred relationship. Our modern definition of covenants as two-way promises between God and man actually misses the heart of covenants. Covenants can create the most binding relationships possible.

We find the same idea in the Book of Mormon. King Benjamin taught his people, "And now, *because of the covenant* which ye have made ye shall be called the *children of Christ, his sons, and his daughters*" (Mosiah 5:7; emphasis added). Did you catch that? A new relationship is established with Christ by means of a covenant. It is potentially the same for each of us.

But what does this mean? How does it work? And what does this have to do with the temple? These are some of the ideas we will explore in this chapter.

Covenant Ceremonies

Anciently, covenants were formed between two or more people through a ceremony.[4] These ceremonies generally included many or all of the following steps:[5]

- An exchange of robes
- An exchange of weapons
- Shedding of blood
- Covenant terms and conditions
- Blessings and penalties for keeping or breaking the covenant
- An exchange of names
- A mark or other token of the covenant
- A covenant meal
- Witnesses of the covenant
- Covenant beneficiaries

Each of these steps was highly symbolic and held great meaning for the participants, the central idea being that of merging or combining identities—of two becoming one. Because of their binding nature, covenants were considered sacred and not entered into lightly. These elements were also found in covenants between God and man. We will discuss each of them and how they might apply to our own gospel covenants.

But first, we must ask: Where did these things come from?

Covenant Origins

In mortality, God originated covenants in the Garden of Eden. Adam and Eve made specific covenants with the Lord and with one another. Later, God made covenants directly with many others, including Enoch, Noah, Melchizedek, Abraham, Isaac, and Jacob.[6]

We also find covenants between individual people early in the biblical record (see Genesis 14:13 and 21:22–34). These covenants between mortals probably modeled those received by man from God, likely containing many of the same elements or ideas. These covenants also established binding relationships between the parties.

As history advanced, covenant relationships spread among most cultures and peoples of the world. Traces of these rites remain scattered throughout the earth, even today.[7] Examining these covenant practices and traditions provides valuable insights into aspects of our own gospel covenants. Let's consider some of the steps associated with covenant ceremonies in ancient times.

The Exchange of Robes

As part of the ceremony, two people entering into a covenant together often exchanged robes or other garments. This practice is illustrated in the biblical story of Jonathan and David.

We read in Samuel that "the soul of Jonathan was knit with the soul of David, and Jonathan loved him as his own soul. . . . Then Jonathan and David made a covenant, because he loved him as his own soul" (1 Samuel 18:1–3). This love describes the kind of relationship that should precede and motivate the making of a covenant. Notice what the record describes next as part of the covenant process. "And Jonathan stripped himself of the robe that was upon him, and gave it to David, and his garments, even to his sword, and to his bow, and to his girdle" (1 Samuel 18:4). We might wonder why, as part of their covenant, Jonathan gave David his robe. What did this exchange symbolize?

Today, we wear mass-produced clothing, but in biblical times, clothes were handmade. Robes were often unique to an individual, especially in the case of someone important like Jonathan. You might have even recognized people from a distance by the robes they wore. Robes could also indicate status.[8] Jonathan was the oldest son of King Saul and heir to the throne. As such, Jonathan's robe undoubtedly identified him.

By giving his robe to David, Jonathan symbolically handed over his identity and status, as the heir to the kingdom, to David.[9] This moment held great symbolic meaning for these two friends. Jonathan's great love for David motivated this exchange. Though we are not told if David did likewise, in many cases both parties exchanged robes, thus sharing or merging their two separate identities into one.

In this, Jonathan stood as a type (or symbol) of the Savior and David as a symbol of each of us. When we accept the gospel and enter into covenants, we are also invited to an exchange of robes. We are offered a chance to exchange the filthiness and nakedness of the natural man and to be clothed by the Lord (see 2 Nephi 9:14; D&C 109:76, 80). Isaiah testified: "I will greatly rejoice in the Lord, my soul shall be joyful in my God; for he hath clothed me with the garments of salvation, *he hath covered me with the robe of righteousness*" (Isaiah 61:10; emphasis added).

For each of us, this exchange can also involve a merging of or an exchange of identities, as the Savior—through the Atonement—was clothed in our sinfulness. "For he hath made him to be sin for us, who knew no sin; that we might be made the righteousness of God in him" (2 Corinthians 5:21). As the Savior assumes our sinfulness, He offers us the opportunity to be clothed in His holiness.

With this idea in mind, consider anew the parable of the prodigal son and how it might apply to our temple ordinances. As you will recall, the younger son eventually came to his senses and decided to return to his father. But while he was still a long ways off, his father saw him and ran to greet and embrace him. The son explained that he had sinned and was no longer worthy to be called a son. Notice what the Father does. He has his servants bring forth his best robe and clothe his son (see Luke 15:11–23). There is great meaning in this simple act of restoring his son's status. Do we see it reflected in our own temple ceremonies?

Along with his robe, Jonathan also gave his weapons and his girdle to David. The girdle referred to is like a sash. In those days, common girdles were made of leather and finer ones from linen (see 2 Kings 1:8; Jeremiah 13:1; Ezekiel 16:10). The girdle confined the flowing robes and often had a sword or dagger suspended from it (see 2 Samuel 20:8; Judges 3:16; Psalm 45:3). Girding up the loins denoted preparation for battle or active exertion. The robes were drawn up under the girdle to allow for running or free movement. Girdles served as a symbol of strength and power (see Isaiah 22:21; 45:5). Righteousness and faithfulness are Christ's girdle (Isaiah 11:5).

Girdles could also serve as pockets or purses for coins. By giving his girdle, Jonathan symbolically pledged his assets to David. What was Jonathan's was now David's. All that rightly belonged to one, the other now had claim upon. Jonathan willingly shared everything with David. His love for David is a beautiful reflection of the Savior's love for us. Like Jonathan, Christ offers us the chance to share in His status as heir to the kingdom.

The Exchange of Weapons

As part of the covenant, Jonathan also gave his sword and bow to David. This represented a pledge of his strength and a promise to safeguard and protect the other, along with an exchange of enemies.[10] David's enemies were now Jonathan's. And Jonathan kept this covenant, even when the *enemy* turned out to be his own father, King Saul.

For example, we learn that Jonathan saved David's life by warning him and helping him hide (1 Samuel 19:2). He defended David verbally before his father and, for a time, softened Saul's heart (1 Samuel 19:4–6). When Saul again turned against David, Jonathan continued to defend him, even at the risk of his own life. At one point, he so angered the king that Saul actually tried to kill Jonathan, who then warned David of the danger with a previously arranged sign of arrows (1 Samuel 20:18–42). Jonathan risked his life to protect his covenant partner.

Both men understood this aspect of their covenants with God as well. David demonstrated it in his response to Goliath. Goliath held the entire army of Israel at bay: "All the men of Israel, when they saw the man, fled from him, and were sore afraid" (1 Samuel 17:24). David responded differently. He asked, "Who is this *uncircumcised* Philistine, that he should defy the armies of the *living* God?" (1 Samuel 17:26, emphasis added).

Circumcision was the mark of the covenant between God and Israel. David understood what it meant to be in a covenant relationship with God. He saw that, by defying the armies of Israel, Goliath defied God as well.[11] And so David accepted the challenge, knowing he had God as his partner. David's older brother was angry at this news and thought David was being a willful, proud, and foolish young man for volunteering to go up against Goliath (1 Samuel 17:28). He saw only the vast gap in the abilities and size of Goliath compared to David.

King Saul also doubted David. David was a shepherd with no experience in war. David recounted to the king how he killed a lion and a bear while tending sheep. He testified, "Thy servant slew both the lion and the bear: and this uncircumcised Philistine shall be as one of them, seeing he hath defied the armies of the living God. . . . The Lord that delivered me out of the paw of the lion, and out of the paw of the bear, he will deliver me out of the hand of this Philistine" (1 Samuel 17:36–37). David again emphasized Goliath's lack of covenant status, as contrasted with his own covenant with the Lord, his confidence stemming from this and his previous experience with God's help.

Goliath's formidable strength and ability represents the arm of flesh. David understood what it meant to go forth in the strength of the Lord (Mosiah 10:10–11). He knew the Lord would protect him and help him to fight his battles. Like Nephi, David recognized that "cursed is he that putteth his trust in the arm of flesh" (2 Nephi 4:34). On the other hand, the Israelite soldiers, like Laman and Lemuel, just couldn't believe that the Lord could be mightier than Laban or Goliath or whatever other challenge loomed in front of them (1 Nephi 3:31). They saw only the obstacle.

But David walked forward in faith. He selected five stones from the brook, indicating that he didn't expect to be successful on the first try. He most likely was prompted by the Holy Ghost and knew that what he was doing was the Lord's will. When we have the reassurance that the Lord is with us and we are doing His will, then our faithfulness to our covenants allows us to expect the Lord's assistance, even by miracles. David demonstrated his understanding by word and deed.

In all of this, Jonathan was not a whit behind David. On one occasion, he and his armor bearer were alone when they came upon a garrison of twenty Philistines. Jonathan stated, "Come, and let us go over unto the garrison of these *uncircumcised*: it may be that *the Lord will work for us*: for there is no restraint to the Lord to save by many or by few" (1 Samuel 14:6; emphasis added). Before proceeding, Jonathan sought and received a sign from the Lord that He was indeed with them (1 Samuel 14:9–10). With this reassurance, Jonathan bravely led the way, and the two proceeded to slay the twenty men with the Lord's aid.

This understanding is important to our faith as well as we confront our own Goliaths. In covenantal language, Paul invited us to take upon ourselves the "whole armour of God," including the "breastplate of righteousness," the "shield of faith," and the "sword of the Spirit" (Ephesians 6:13–17). As covenant partners, God will be our strength (2 Nephi 22:2).

Our enemies—Satan, death, sin, and the natural man—become the Lord's enemies as well. In the strength of the Lord, we shall contend against our enemies (see Words of Mormon 1:14). Those not in the covenant are left to their own strength (Mosiah 10:11). Indeed, Paul testified that the Lord's people can do all things through Him (see Philippians 4:13).

Of course, the Lord permits us to be tried and tested. He allows failure, setbacks, heartaches, disappointments, and opposition as we need—and as He sees fit (see Mosiah 3:19). Even the Savior was not exempt from these things. But we have the assurance that, as we are faithful, these will all be temporary. The ultimate outcome is without doubt (see D&C 122:7–9).

Like Nephi, at times we may be given strength to break our bands (1 Nephi 7:18), while at other times we will be subject to them (1 Nephi 18:15), according to the Lord's will. Do not fear your Goliaths. Let them build and strengthen your faith.

Consider these words—and remember they are the Lord's— from the dedication of the Kirtland Temple:

> We ask thee, Holy Father, to establish the people that shall worship, and honorably hold a name and standing in this thy house, to all generations and for eternity;
>
> That no weapon formed against them shall prosper; that he who diggeth a pit for them shall fall into the same himself;
>
> That no combination of wickedness shall have power to rise up and prevail over thy people upon whom thy name shall be put in this house;
>
> And if any people shall rise against this people, that thine anger be kindled against them;
>
> And if they shall smite this people thou wilt smite them; thou wilt fight for thy people as thou didst in the day of battle, that they may be delivered from the hands of all their enemies.[12]

The Shedding of Blood

Among ancient peoples, the shedding of blood sealed a covenant. This was generally done with proxy or substitute blood through the sacrifice of an animal. The animal stood as a representative of the two parties. To finalize the agreement, its throat was slit and its blood spilt. The animal was then used as the main dish in a ceremonial meal. Other cultures sometimes entered directly into a covenant with their own blood. These "blood covenants"[13] were considered the most binding union possible. Such covenants were accomplished in various ways. One method was by making an incision in the hand, wrist, or arm of each person, and then pressing the cuts together, allowing the blood to mingle between the two friends.[14] The two thus became "blood brothers."

Blood represents life (see Leviticus 17:11–14). Shedding blood signified that the life of the one covenanting was devoted or surrendered to the other party.[15] The exchange of blood represented the transfer of life itself.[16] By sharing or mingling blood, both parties fused their two lives and separate identities into one.

Once formed, such a covenant created a bond considered unbreakable, and from which neither party could be released.[17] Our modern day saying of "blood is thicker than water" descends from this idea. In other words, the blood of the covenant is thicker, or creates a stronger bond, than the waters of birth, meaning the bond between blood brothers is closer and more binding than even that of siblings from the same mother.[18]

The Hebrew word for covenant, *be'rith*, refers to something cut.[19] The Old Testament phrase for making a covenant is *karat be'rith*, meaning literally to "cut a covenant" or "cut a bond." Blood (life) had to be shed for a covenant to be binding.[20]

Blood is sometimes required in gospel covenants too. When God established a covenant with Abraham concerning his seed, He required some of Abraham's blood at the source of his paternity through the rite of circumcision, symbolizing, among other things, that his posterity would be dedicated or surrendered to the Lord. God required this token and covenant of Abraham's descendants as well (see Genesis 17). So serious was the Lord about this that any who were not circumcised were cut off from the Lord's people and were considered to have broken the covenant (see Genesis 17:14).

Christ establishes His covenant with us not vicariously, but with His own blood. It is His "blood that maketh an atonement for the soul" (Leviticus 17:11). This was not, however, merely a cut on the palm of His hand or wrist, though His hands and wrists were pierced. Nor was it a quick slitting of the throat, as in the case of the sacrificial animals. The burden placed upon Him was so great that blood was wrung from His every pore (see Mosiah 3:7). "Which suffering caused myself, even God, the greatest of all, to tremble because of pain, and to bleed at every pore, and to suffer both body and spirit" (D&C 19:18). We are not bought with something perishable, like silver or gold, but with the precious blood of Christ (see 1 Peter 1:18–19).

From Adam until Christ, men offered up sacrifices from their flocks.[21] This was in similitude of the Savior's great atoning sacrifice (see Moses 5:7). It served to teach and remind them of God's sacrifice for, love of, and covenant and relationship with them.

During past ages when economic livelihood often depended upon animals, the offering of an unblemished male bullock or ram represented a real sacrifice on the part of the one making the offering. A perfect male animal could provide future breeding stock, helping to ensure the health of the herd. It also represented food and clothing for the family. In light of this, and in a much smaller way, the sacrificial animal also symbolized the surrendering and devotion of the life of the one making the sacrifice unto God. For those who understood, offering such a sacrifice was not just a gift offered unto the Lord, it was also a token of the Lord's commitment to that person's redemption and that person's commitment in return to the Lord.

Abel offered a sacrifice and was accepted. Cain also offered a sacrifice, but it was not accepted (see Genesis 4:2–5).[22] The biblical narrative "shows Abel lovingly and trustfully reaching out to God with substitute blood, in order to be in covenant oneness with God; while Cain merely proffers a gift from his earthly possessions. Abel so trusts God that he gives *himself* to Him. Cain defers to God sufficiently to make a *present* to Him."[23]

With these ideas in mind, we might wonder if mortal man has ever entered into anything akin to a blood covenant with Deity?[24] Interestingly, we find something similar when Moses and the Israelites made a covenant with the Lord.[25] After the children of Israel arrived at Mount Sinai in the wilderness, they were told to sanctify themselves for three days. The Lord then descended upon the mount in smoke and fire (see Exodus 19:20). From the mount, though hidden from view, God spoke to all the people, giving them the Ten Commandments as part of the covenant He would make with them (Exodus 20:1–17, 22; Exodus 19:9). "And the sight of the glory of the Lord was like devouring fire on the top of the mount in the eyes of the children of Israel" (Exodus 24:17). The people shrank from this encounter and asked

Moses to speak with God on their behalf (Exodus 20:19). Moses told them not to fear and that the manifestation was for their benefit so that they would have respect for the Lord and refrain from sin (Exodus 20:20).

Moses wrote the words of the Lord (Exodus 24:4). After the people committed to doing all that the Lord had commanded (Exodus 24:3), Moses then constructed an altar from unhewn stone, as he had been instructed. The unhewn stone was important because the altar was to represent the Lord. "For if thou lift up thy tool upon it, thou hast polluted it" (Exodus 25:20 also see Exodus 24:4). Moses also erected twelve pillars to serve as witnesses to the covenant, one for each of the tribes (Exodus 24:4).

Oxen were sacrificed as peace offerings unto the Lord. Their blood was shed to seal the covenant. Half of the blood from these animals Moses sprinkled upon the altar, representing God. The other half he caught in basins and sprinkled upon the people, saying, "Behold the blood of the covenant, which the Lord hath made with you concerning all these words" (Exodus 24:8). The Lord had stated that He would be their God and they would be His people (see Leviticus 26:12; 2 Corinthians 6:16). This sacred relationship was established through covenant ritual.

Following this covenant ceremony, Moses, Aaron, Nadab, Abihu, and seventy of the elders of Israel entered into the Lord's presence. "And they saw the God of Israel: and there was under his feet as it were a paved work of a sapphire stone, and as it were the body of heaven in his clearness" (Exodus 24:10). In this sacred setting, they then shared a covenantal meal (see Exodus 24:11).

After the Savior's sacrifice, He discontinued the shedding of blood. Nevertheless, covenants are still established through sacrifice (see Psalm 50:5; D&C 97:8; 138:13). We are now commanded to offer, as a sacrifice, a broken heart and a contrite spirit (see 3 Nephi 9:19–20; Omni 1:26; D&C 64:34). It is our pride, rebellion, stubbornness, and will that is to be sacrificed. It is not to be a symbolic gift, but a real and personal offering. How much more difficult is this than sacrificing an animal? We are to be circumcised in our hearts (see 2 Nephi 9:33; Romans 2:28–29; Acts 7:51; Ezekiel 44:9; Deuteronomy 10:14–16; 30:1–6). Our garments are to be washed white through His blood (see 1 Nephi 12:10; Alma 5:21; 13:11–13; 3 Nephi 27:19–20). We are to surrender ourselves unto our Savior. Only then can His sacrifice bring about our "at-one-ment" and reconciliation with the Father.

Covenant Terms and Conditions

As part of a covenant, each party also agreed to keep certain terms and conditions. This is where we get our notion of covenants as two-way promises.

Only God can make and offer a covenant that will endure beyond the grave and into eternity (see D&C 132:7). He alone sets the terms. We are free to accept or reject the covenant offered, but we do not set the terms. Though man may break covenants, God never will (see D&C 109:1). "What I the Lord have spoken, I have spoken, and I excuse not myself; and though the heavens and the earth pass away, my word shall not pass away, but shall all be fulfilled" (D&C 1:38). As a result, gospel covenants are given to us conditionally, based upon our subsequent faithfulness. Many of the terms are outlined in the scriptures.

Both the Hebrew and Greek words for *testament* can also be translated as "covenant." Thus, the Old Testament could be appropriately entitled the Old Covenant and the New Testament could be entitled the New Covenant.

In the Old Testament, the Ten Commandments were not merely commandments; they were part of the terms and conditions of the covenant between God and His people, Israel (Deuteronomy 5:1–27). The stone tablets containing these commandments were called the tablets of the covenant (Deuteronomy 9:15). They were housed in the ark of the covenant.

Understanding these commandments as part of the covenant terms between the Lord and His people can enhance our understanding of their purpose and meaning. For example, the commandment to not take the Lord's name in vain is far more than a prohibition against swearing, as is commonly taught. It is an admonition to not enter into covenant relationship lightly or without intent to fulfill our obligations. Once in covenant, we represent Him and must bear His name in reverence and sincerity before the world. We take the Lord's name in vain if we preach false and foolish doctrine or the philosophies of men in His name. Our works should rather glorify His name by reflecting His will in our lives.[26]

Many understand the *old covenant* to be about works and justice and the law of Moses. Some suppose that this *old covenant* was replaced with the *new covenant* of salvation by grace. While it is overwhelmingly true that we are saved by grace (2 Nephi 25:23) and that Christ's grace shields us from full exposure to the law (see Romans 6:14; 10:4; Galatians 2:16; 3:13; James 2:10), such grace does not fully remove our covenant responsibility. Contrary to the notion that the strict Ten Commandments and law of Moses were replaced by an easier way, Christ actually raised the bar. Those who believe otherwise do not understand his Sermon on the Mount. This sermon contains the terms of His *new covenant.*

Christ moved the battle from merely controlling one's actions to mastering one's heart, thoughts, and emotions. Rather than simply refraining from killing, disciples are to forsake anger (3 Nephi 12:21–22). Not only is adultery (fornication) forbidden, so are lustful thoughts (3 Nephi 12:27–29). Those wronged are not to seek justice, or an "eye for an eye," but are to forgive and turn the other cheek. We are to return good for evil and love our enemies (3 Nephi 12:39–44). Such was the character of our Savior, and such are the demands of His *new covenant.*[27] "When men are called unto mine everlasting gospel, and covenant with an everlasting covenant, they are accounted as the salt of the earth and the savor of men; they are called to be the savor of men; therefore, if that salt of the earth lose its savor, behold, it is thenceforth good for nothing only to be cast out and trodden under the feet of men" (D&C 101:39–40).

Blessings and Penalties

Along with the terms and conditions, covenants also include certain blessings for keeping them and penalties for breaking them. With most gospel covenants, we focus on and understand the attached blessings. Some of these blessings are immediate; others may be reserved for the future. But what about the penalties?

There was an incident in Abraham's life that illustrates the understanding ancient peoples had of covenant penalties. It helps us to see the seriousness of a covenant relationship. We read in JST Genesis 15:7–18.[28]

7 And the Lord said unto him, I am the Lord that brought thee out of
Ur of the Chaldees, to give thee this land to inherit it.
8 And Abram said, Lord God, whereby shall I know that I shall inherit
it? Yet he believed God.

Abraham's question here does not appear to be motivated by
doubt.[29] The Spirit likely prompted his question. The Lord was using
the occasion to teach him.

9 And the Lord said unto him, Take me an heifer of three years old, and a
she goat of three years old, and a ram of three years old, and a turtledove,
and a young pigeon.

At three years old, these animals were considered fully grown and
in their prime. It is interesting that every animal allowed or commanded to be sacrificed under the future Mosaic law can be found
on this list. Hebrew *meshullash* (translated as "three years old") may
also mean "threefold," referring to three of each species. Either way,
in this case, three seems to be symbolic of the Godhead.

10 And he took unto him all these, and he divided them in the midst,
and he laid each piece one against the other: but the birds divided
he not.

Abraham took the animals, killed them, and cut them in half
along the spine, from the head to the end. He then arranged the pieces
opposite each other in pairs, forming a pathway down the center. As
the pieces drained, blood pooled into this pathway.[30]

Abraham understood the significance of what he was doing. In
ancient cultures, this was a well-established means to ratify a covenant.
Once a covenant and its terms were agreed to, the two parties walked
through the blood path as a way of agreeing to keep the terms and accepting the penalty if they failed. In essence, they were saying, "May what
was done to these animals be done to me if I fail to keep this covenant."[31]

A clear biblical example of this type of penalty is found in Jeremiah,
where the Lord states: "And I will give the men that have transgressed
my covenant, which have not performed the words of the covenant
which they had made before me, when they cut the calf in twain, and
passed between the parts thereof. . . . I will even give them into the
hand of their enemies, and into the hand of them that seek their life:

and their dead bodies shall be for meat unto the fowls of the heaven, and to the beasts of the earth."[32]

Continuing with the account of Abraham, we read:

> 11 And when the fowls came down upon the carcasses, Abram drove them away.[33]
> 12 And when the sun was going down, a deep sleep fell upon Abram; and lo, a great horror of great darkness fell upon him.

The deep sleep referred to here indicates a visionary experience, not slumber (see, for example, Daniel 8:18; 10:9). The horror of great darkness may have been a vision to Abraham of the torment of the sons of perdition (see D&C 76:47). As such, it represented the Lord's penalty if He failed to fulfill His covenant to Abram. Obviously, God cannot be torn asunder as the beasts that were sacrificed. However, Alma taught that under certain conditions, God could cease to be God (Alma 42:22–25). If that were to occur, God would become perdition.

God has said that His words cannot return void (unfulfilled), "for as they go forth out of my mouth they must be fulfilled" (Moses 4:30). In this instance, God was giving Abraham a visible example, in terms that Abraham understood. In making this covenant, God was placing His Godhood on the line. What greater witness could He have given Abraham (in answer to his query from verse 8)?

> 13 And the Lord spake, and he said unto Abram, Know of a surety that thy seed shall be a stranger in a land which shall not be theirs, and shall serve strangers; and they shall be afflicted and serve them four hundred years;
> 14 And also that nation, whom they shall serve, will I judge: and afterwards shall they come out with great substance.
> 15 And thou shalt die and go to thy fathers in peace; thou shalt be buried in good old age.
> 16 But in the fourth generation they shall come hither again: for the iniquity of the Amorites is not yet full.
> 17 And it came to pass, that, when the sun went down, and it was dark, behold a smoking furnace, and a burning lamp that passed between those pieces which Abram had divided.

The smoking furnace and the burning lamp both represented the Lord (see Exodus 13:21; 14:24; 19:18; 20:18; Isaiah 6:4; Hebrews

12:29; Revelations 15:8). Customarily, the greater of the two parties walked on the blood path first. The Lord, as the smoking furnace, passed first through the blood path. Then, at the point in which Abraham would normally have walked the path as the lesser of the two parties, the Lord again passed through the path, this time as a burning lamp.

This was a unilateral covenant. The Lord was making it to Abraham and would hold Himself to it. Abraham was not responsible for its fulfillment. It was solely up to God to implement the promise of descendants and land.

> 18 And in that same day the Lord made a covenant with Abram, saying, Unto thy seed have I given this land, from the river of Egypt unto the great river, the river Euphrates.

From this incident, we are given a sense of the gravity of God's covenants to us and ours with Him. They are not to be taken or entered into lightly. The Bible contains a number of examples of penalties incurred by men and women who broke their covenants.[34]

We also find covenant penalties in the Book of Mormon. When Moroni raised the title of liberty to rally his people, their response is interesting: "And it came to pass that when Moroni had proclaimed these words, behold, the people came running together with their armor girded about their loins, rending their garments in token, or as a covenant, that they would not forsake the Lord their God; or, in other words, if they should transgress the commandments of God, or fall into transgression, and be ashamed to take upon them the name of Christ, the Lord should rend them even as they had rent their garments" (Alma 46:21).

While it is important to realize the seriousness of covenants, it is also good to remember that the Lord is merciful unto us. He keeps His covenants perfectly. We don't walk perfectly as He does. He holds Himself to an exacting standard and will fulfill every whit. The gospel for us involves learning and progression. Even the best of us fall short. Despite our failures, our efforts to keep our covenants can be accepted. The Lord reminds us that He keeps His covenants and shows mercy "unto thy servants who walk uprightly before thee, with all their hearts" (D&C 109:1). We generally know when our hearts are right before the Lord and when they are not. Through the Atonement and the ordinance of the sacrament, the Lord blesses and covers us as we repent and seek to make our covenants part of our character.

"Behold, the Lord requireth the heart and a willing mind" (D&C 64:34). And again, "Verily I say unto you, all among them who *know* their hearts are honest, and are broken, and their spirits contrite, and are *willing* to observe their covenants by sacrifice—yea, every sacrifice which I, the Lord, shall command—they are accepted of me" (D&C 97:8; emphasis added).

The Exchange of Names

Another step in a covenant ceremony was often an exchange of names. In our society, names are generally little more than identifiers. In the Book of Mormon, Helaman gave his sons Nephi and Lehi their names to be a positive, molding influence in their lives (see Helaman 5:6–7). We likewise may be named for ancestors or scriptural characters, but in many instances, names in our society don't convey meanings.

In the ancient Near East, names were thought to be extremely powerful.[35] It was believed that a name captured the essence of an individual. There was an intimate connection between naming and existence. In some ways, names were viewed as a separate manifestation of a person or deity.

A man or woman was not complete until named because they were composed of body, soul, and name.[36] Renaming or giving a new name could indicate rebirth or adoption into a new household, or a change of status or position, along with accompanying responsibilities and privileges.[37]

Through the restored gospel, we learn that Michael became Adam on this earth. His new name indicated his changed status. In Hebrew, names generally have meaning. The name *Adam* contains the root Hebrew word *dam,* meaning "blood." So in Adam's name, there is a reminder of the Fall, life, and death. The letter *a* (*aleph*) that precedes *dam* connotes teaching or leadership, implying—in the name *Adam*—that man is to learn to control and discipline his nature and is given the ability to act and not simply be acted upon.

Adam is also related to *adama,* meaning "earth," and could be interpreted as "of the earth," capturing in his name the idea that Adam was created from the dust of the earth and was sentenced to return to it. But in this there was hope, as dust also represents the ground, which can be planted to bring forth new life and eventually bear fruit. So, in addition to the Fall and his return to the dust, Adam's name also pointed to his potential for growth and redemption.

In a blood covenant, each party took a portion of the other's name as their own.[38] This again symbolized the joining of two lives into one, and it identified to others the covenant partner. By way of example, if two men entered into such a covenant, one named John Smith and the other Henry Walker, they might have been known thereafter as John Henry Smith and Henry John Walker. Their new names indicated their covenant status and covenant partner. In our culture, we follow a similar custom at marriage, when a wife takes the surname of her husband.

How does this relate to the gospel? In Genesis, we read, "And when Abram was ninety years old and nine, the Lord appeared to Abram, and said unto him, I am the Almighty God; walk before me, and be thou perfect. And I will make my covenant between me and thee, and will multiply thee exceedingly. . . . Neither shall thy name any more be called Abram, but thy name shall be Abraham; for a father of many nations have I made thee. . . . As for Sarai thy wife, thou shalt not call her name Sarai, but Sarah shall her name be" (Genesis 17:1–2, 5, 15).

This change of name denoted a change of status for Abraham. But it was also a token of the covenant and his covenant partner. Jehovah gave Abram part of His own name. The letter *h* from the Hebrew *YHWH* was added to Abram, and his name was changed to AbraHam. Sarai became SaraH. The meaning of Abram, being "a high father," was changed to Abraham, or "father of a multitude of nations."

But what is interesting is that the Lord also assumed Abraham's name. Thereafter in the biblical record, He often referred to Himself as the God of Abraham. This gives us a sense of the relationship that the Lord had with Abraham—and a glimpse of the type of relationship He desires with Abraham's posterity, including those adopted into the line, meaning us.

Throughout the scriptures, we read of becoming a son (or daughter) of God (for examples, see 3 Nephi 9:17; Moroni 7:26, 48; D&C

11:30; 35:2; 45:8; 76:58). Stop a minute and think about that. *Becoming* a son or daughter of God? Aren't we already His sons and daughters? What do the scriptures mean, which teach we must *become* a son or daughter of God?

We find an answer in the vision given to Joseph Smith and Sidney Rigdon. Speaking of those who inherit celestial glory, it states, "Wherefore, as it is written, they are gods, even the sons of God"(D&C 76:58). Despite the fact that you are a spirit son or daughter of heavenly parents, you must also be adopted into the exalted family of God as His son or His daughter. This occurs through covenant, as the Father accepts you into His eternal family as an heir.

The opening chapter of the Book of Mormon contains an example of this. Lehi saw the Father sitting upon His throne, surrounded by angels who were singing and praising *their* god (see 1 Nephi 1:8). Lehi saw these angels but is not included as part of the group. After being ministered to by Christ, Lehi's status changed. And Lehi joined the angels "in the praising of *his* God" (1 Nephi 1:15; emphasis added).

What changed? Why did Lehi begin to refer to God as "his"? The answer isn't apparent until many chapters later, when we learn that God entered into covenant with Lehi (see 2 Nephi 1:5). It is through a direct covenant relationship that we become sons or daughters of God—or members of His eternal family. It is in this sense that Jehovah became "the God of Abraham, the God of Isaac, and the God of Jacob" (see Exodus 3:6). Each received his or her own covenant directly from God. We must do the same.

Jacob received his new name, Israel, as part of the blessing he received when he wrestled (or embraced) the Lord and entered into His presence (see Genesis 32:24, 27–30). Jacob then named the holy place Peniel (meaning "face of God"), testifying that he had seen God's face and lived (see Genesis 32:30). Near the end of his life, Jacob equated the blessings he received from the Lord with the new name he received (see Genesis 48:16).

God also covenanted with Lehi. We are not told his new name, but the Father and the Son became "his God" in the same manner. And it is this same covenantal relationship that allowed Nephi to later speak of Jesus as being "*my* Jesus" (see 2 Nephi 33:6; emphasis added).

At some point, our spiritual rebirth will likewise involve receiving a new name as we are begotten sons and daughters unto God and as He claims us (see D&C 130:11).

Our own temple covenants testify of these things. In them is an invitation for you to likewise become a son or daughter of God. Recognize, though, that Lehi did not receive this covenant from an earthly ordinance. Nor did Abraham, Isaac, Jacob, or Nephi. They received it directly from God. We are invited to do the same: "Wherefore, all men must take upon them the name *which is given of the Father*, for in that name shall they be called at the last day; wherefore, if they know not the name by which they are called, they cannot have place in the kingdom of my Father" (D&C 18:24–25 emphasis added).

Covenant Marks or Tokens

Many times, covenant ceremonies left a mark on the body, or some other token of the covenant. For example, in blood covenants, after making an incision in the palm or wrist, the two parties clasped hands or forearms to allow their blood to flow together. Afterward, an abrasive substance was sometimes rubbed into the wound to leave a permanent mark or scar as a token of the covenant. Thereafter, when either party wanted to disclose their covenant status, hands and arms were raised to display these marks. It may be that our handshake, used when reaching a deal, and practice of waving in greeting both descend from these older customs.[39]

Sometimes other tokens were used. Something stained by the covenant blood was often kept as a record of the covenant (see Hebrews 9:19). This could be sewn into a leather case and worn as an armband or necklace. In a covenant between a man and a woman, blood was generally not shared, but a bracelet was given and worn as a reminder of being bound together in a covenant bond. This *bracelet-binding* held a similar idea to *blood-binding*.[40]

Something like this may have been behind the gift of two bracelets to Rebekah on behalf of Isaac by Abraham's steward (see Genesis 24:22). The steward had previously asked God for a sign to indicate the right woman. When Rebekah met the steward, he offered the symbolic gifts to her, even before meeting her father and arranging the terms of the marriage. Rebekah likely understood the significance of the bracelets. Today, we exchange rings instead of bracelets, but they also serve as tokens of a marriage covenant.

In our gospel covenants, marks and tokens are important.[41] Circumcision was the mark of the covenant between God, Abraham, and his posterity (see Genesis 17:10). Though this was a physical token, it was intended to represent something spiritual, a commitment on the part of the marked individual (see Jeremiah 4:4). Despite this outward mark, it was the individual's heart that was to be circumcised and of which primarily concerned the Lord (see Deuteronomy 10:16; Romans 2:27–29; Colossians 2:11).

Our heart represents our desires, motives, and passions. Circumcising one's heart is aligning our will with God's and keeping our appetites and desires within His boundaries. Without a circumcised heart, the physical rite of circumcision was ultimately meaningless (see Jeremiah 9:25). The Book of Mormon cautions, "Wo unto the uncircumcised of heart, for a knowledge of their iniquities shall smite them at the last day" (2 Nephi 9:33). Those with uncircumcised hearts do not have their covenants written in their hearts.

Our Savior bears covenantal marks on his body. Isaiah testified, "Can a woman forget her sucking child, that she should not have compassion on the son of her womb? yea, they may forget, yet will I not forget thee. Behold, *I have graven thee upon the palms of my hands*; thy walls are continually before me" (Isaiah 49:15–16; emphasis added). We also bear covenantal marks. Not in our flesh, but nevertheless upon our person as we wear our garments.

The Covenantal Meal

As the ceremony concluded, the participants often shared a meal to seal and celebrate their covenant. Generally, this feast was the sacrificial animal. It represented both parties, and the two covenant partners often fed each other the first few bites, symbolizing once again the surrendering of their lives to one another and the joining of the two into one.[42] We witness something similar, perhaps without recognizing the symbolism, when a bride and a groom feed one another the first bite of cake at the end of their wedding ceremony. By this action, the groom symbolically gives himself to his bride, and the bride does likewise. The two are becoming one.

In the gospel, we participate in a covenantal meal through the sacrament. On one occasion during His ministry, the Savior fed five thousand people by providing bread through miraculous means (see John 6). Because of this miracle, the people perceived Him to be a prophet and wanted to make Him their king. As the day drew to a close, He dismissed the multitude, put His disciples in a boat, and departed into a mountain alone. The following day, when the people returned and couldn't find Him, they entered into boats and crossed over to Capernaum, seeking Him. When they found Him, He gave them a clear statement of who He truly was in a discourse on the Bread of Life (see John 6:26–58).

Christ is the sacrificial lamb. He is the Bread of Life, the true manna from heaven. These Jews feigned ignorance, but they understood what he was teaching. This discourse was a plain statement of His identity. They understood it, but they would not believe or accept it. The scriptures record that "from that time many of his disciples went back, and walked no more with him" (John 6:66). They could accept Him as a prophet or a king, but not as the Messiah. He didn't fit their image of what the Messiah should have been.

Consider a portion of His words on that occasion, in the context of covenantal imagery.

> I am the living bread which came down from heaven: if any man eat of this bread, he shall live for ever: and the bread that I will give is my flesh, which I will give for the life of the world. The Jews therefore strove among themselves, saying, how can this man give us his flesh to eat? Then Jesus said unto them, Verily, verily, I say unto you, except ye eat the flesh of the Son of man, and drink his blood, ye have no life in you. Whoso eateth my flesh, and drinketh my blood, hath eternal life; and I will raise him up at the last day. For my flesh is meat indeed, and my blood is drink indeed. He that eateth my flesh, and drinketh my blood, *dwelleth in me, and I in him.* (John 6:51–56, emphasis added)

It was at the Last Supper that the Savior introduced the sacrament. The occasion was the Passover, which symbolized, through ritual, Israel's deliverance from Egypt, and looked back in remembrance of God's great blessings. But more than that, for those with eyes to see, the Passover was also filled with symbols pointing forward to the Savior's future role as the Redeemer.

The whole Passover experience provided a beautiful type of Christ. Ancient Israel labored in physical bondage. The blood of the lamb smeared upon their doorposts saved them from death.[43] They were delivered out of physical bondage by the Lord's hand. They were sustained by bread from heaven (manna) during their journey in the wilderness until they were at last brought into the promised land.

Manna represented Christ. It was the symbol. He was the real thing. He was the living bread come down from heaven.

Like ancient Israel, we are fallen, temporally and spiritually. We all find ourselves in bondage of some form. Our deliverance likewise comes through Christ. The blood of the Lamb saves us from death. Our journey in the wilderness of life is likewise sustained by bread from heaven (the sacrament). And Christ intends to lead us to a promised land (heaven).

How does Christ's statement, "He that eateth my flesh, and drinketh my blood, dwelleth in me, and I in him" (John 6:56) relate to our sacrament prayers and our own covenant with Him? How might it relate to hungering and thirsting after righteousness and being filled (see 3 Nephi 12:6)?

May we approach the sacrament each week with greater reverence. Can we come to the feast of the Lord holding a grudge against another who may also have come to the table?

One December, I realized I had been doing exactly that. My heart held grudges and nursed past injuries. Some were petty; stupid bumps and bruises in the normal course of life that should not have been allowed to fester. Others were wounds inflicted on my family and myself that truly were unjust.

As Christmas approached, I pondered upon what gift I could give my Savior. I felt impressed that my gift should be to lay these burdens at His feet and forgive those who had injured me. In doing so, I intended to give a gift but found instead that I was the one who was blessed. Little had I realized what a heavy load I was carrying until I finally set it down and tried to forgive with all my heart. It wasn't easy, but I sought small ways to serve them and pray for them.

That month, the sacrament truly became a spiritual feast. I received forgiveness for my own sins and learned the truth in the Savior's prayer: "forgive us our debts, as we forgive our debtors" (Matthew 5:12). That principle is not simply an ideal to strive for. It truly is the key that frees the Lord to forgive us. May we come to the sacrament table, to our covenant meal, with repentant and forgiving hearts and clean hands so that He may dwell in us, and we in Him.

Witnesses of the Covenant

Covenants generally required one or more witnesses. Sometimes a monument was erected as a physical reminder. In the Bible, rocks and trees were commonly used as such,[44] in part because they have a degree of permanence and would remain in place beyond the lives of the original covenantal parties. Both held symbolic meaning as well.

Jacob and Laban used a pillar or heap of stones as a witness of their covenant (see Genesis 31:44–55). These stones not only stood as a reminder, but they also formed a boundary. Neither party was to pass the heap of stones with the intent to harm the other (see Genesis 31:52).

This heap of stones was likely an altar. Jacob and Laban shared a covenant meal upon the heap (see Genesis 31:46), likely a sacrificial animal. This altar represented the Lord (see 1 Samuel 2:2; Deuteronomy 32:4; D&C 50:44), who was to continue to watch over the two parties once they parted (see Genesis 31:49).

Stone altars are an appropriate witness to a covenant as they point to our Savior. One of Christ's titles is the "Rock of Heaven" (Moses 7:53). He is the rock upon which we are to build (see Helaman 5:12); the rock of our salvation (see 2 Nephi 9:45); the rock from which we are hewn (see 2 Nephi 8:1); the rock that brings forth living water (see 2 Nephi 25:20; 1 Corinthians 10:4); the chief corner stone (see Ephesians 2:20); the stone that the builders rejected (see Matthew 21:42); and the stone of Israel (see Genesis 35:14).

When Joshua and the Israelites crossed the river Jordan and entered into the promised land, just as the Lord had covenanted with Abraham centuries earlier, the Lord commanded Joshua to have twelve stones carried from the riverbed and piled in a heap on the other side as a memorial. This heap was a reminder of the miraculous crossing and God's covenant fulfilled. It was to be a witness to future generations. "This may be a sign among you, that when your children ask their fathers in time to come, saying, what mean ye by these stones? Then ye shall answer them . . . and these stones shall be for a memorial unto the children of Israel for ever" (Joshua 4:6–7; see 1–9).

Joshua challenged Israel to remain faithful to God with his well-known words: "Choose you this day whom ye will serve" (Joshua 24:15). After the people said they would serve God, it is interesting to note that Joshua put them under covenant on that day. Following that, he took a great stone and set it up under an oak tree next to the tabernacle. "And Joshua said unto all the people, Behold, this stone shall be a witness unto us; for it hath heard all the words of the Lord which he spake unto us: it shall be therefore a witness unto you, lest ye deny your God" (Joshua 24:27). Here, both a stone and a tree are used as covenant witnesses.

Earlier in the biblical record, we find a tree being utilized as a witness in the covenant between Abraham and Abimelech. When conflict broke out over a well, Abimelech and Abraham made a covenant treaty. Abimelech desired the agreement to be multi-generational, extending to his son and his grandson (see Genesis 21:23). As a witness to their covenant, Abimelech planted a tamarisk tree in Beer-sheba and called upon the name of the Lord (see JST Genesis 21:31). This tree would stand as a reminder to their posterity.

The idea of a tree as a covenant witness or symbol is appropriate in a gospel context and points to three other gospel trees. The first tree is the tree of knowledge of good and evil. One of our purposes in coming to this earth is to partake of this tree ourselves—we learn to distinguish between good and evil by our own experiences. When Adam and Eve partook, they were driven from the Garden of Eden (the world's first temple) and cherubim were placed to guard the way back to the tree of life (see Genesis 3:23–24). There was time and space given unto man to repent and learn what is needed (see Alma 42:4).

The Savior opened the way for our return as He redeemed us, first in the Garden of Gethsemane, where trees witnessed His Atonement, and then on the tree from which He hung as He suffered the Crucifixion.

These three trees (the tree of knowledge, the tree of the cross, and the tree of life) form a beautiful chiasmus, symbolizing our departure from, redemption by, and return to God. Trees, therefore, are fitting symbols of our covenant partnership with the Savior.

Furthering this symbolism, trees are not created by man. With all of our science and technology, humans cannot create seeds, let alone a sprout or even a tree. We can plant and nurture, but it is the Lord that causes the growth. We merely share in the fruits (see Alma 32:28–43).

The Lord has likened us to trees. He promises that as we keep our covenants: "I, the Lord, will cause them to bring forth as a very fruitful tree which is planted in a goodly land, by a pure stream, that yieldeth much precious fruit" (D&C 97:9). And again, in this caution, the "ax is laid at the root of the trees; and every tree that bringeth not forth good fruit shall be hewn down and cast into the fire" (D&C 97:7).

Today, temples stand as visible reminders of and monuments to our covenants. May we live so that not only the temples, but also our lives are monuments to our covenants.

Covenant Beneficiaries

Anciently covenants often extended beyond the lives of the original parties to include their descendants. We find an example of this in the covenant between David and Jonathan. Following the deaths of King Saul and Jonathan, a prolonged war erupted between the remaining house of Saul and the house of David (see 2 Samuel 3:1). After prevailing in this conflict and becoming king, David lamented, "Is there yet any that is left of the house of Saul, that I may shew him kindness *for Jonathan's sake?*" (2 Samuel 9:1; emphasis added). A search did reveal that one of Jonathan's sons still lived (see 2 Samuel 9:3).

Mephibosheth, born Merib-baal, was but five years old when his father died. His nurse, fearing for his life, fled with the young boy. In their haste, an accident left Merib-baal lame in both feet. As a result, he became known as Mephibosheth (meaning "shameful thing"). King David, learning of Jonathan's lame son, caused him to be brought forth to his court. This must have been terrifying to Mephibosheth, who likely esteemed David as an enemy because of the long war with the house of Saul. He may have feared for his life and was probably unaware of the earlier covenant between David and his father.

When Mephibosheth arrived in Jerusalem, David greeted him, saying, "Fear not: for I will surely shew thee kindness for Jonathan thy father's sake" (2 Samuel 9:7). The king then brought Mephibosheth to his own table to eat as one of his own sons and restored to him all of the lands of Saul (2 Samuel 9:9–13). Mephibosheth marveled at this, exclaiming, "What is thy servant, that thou shouldest look upon such a dead dog as I am?" (2 Samuel 9:8). How could this be? Mephibosheth didn't understand. Here was his grandfather's enemy and rival to the throne. And yet King David is bringing him—a lame, shameful thing—into his house as one of his own sons. David did this for Jonathan's sake, not for any merit on Mephibosheth's part.

In this story, we see a beautiful type. Earlier in their covenant, Jonathan's love for David mirrored the Savior's great love for us. Now King David's actions become a type of the Father. For the sake of His Beloved Son (Jonathan), the Father (David) extends grace to us (as Mephibosheth) as a result of the Savior's sacrifice and His covenant with us. We too, through Christ's merits, may be restored to our Father's table (see 2 Nephi 2:8; 31:19; Moroni 6:4; D&C 3:20).

Conclusion

Covenants are a serious matter with the Lord. We see this in the dedicatory prayer of the Kirtland Temple. This prayer was given by revelation. The words are the Lord's and have significance. It began by stating: "Thanks be to thy name, O Lord God of Israel, *who keepest covenant*" (D&C 109:1; emphasis added). Of all God's titles and of all the ways He could be addressed, here at the dedication of the first temple of the Restoration, He chose to remind us and to be known as One who keeps His covenants!

We find another example of how the Lord views covenants as the ancient Israelites concluded their wandering in the wilderness and entered the promised land (see Joshua 9–10). Israel had begun destroying the existing inhabitants as commanded by the Lord. Upon hearing of the annihilation of both Jericho and Ai, the people of Gibeon were deathly afraid of the Israelites and realized it was only a matter of time before they met the same fate. Recognizing they would not prevail in a fight, they resolved upon a strategy to save their lives.

So the Gibeonites sent an embassy to the Israelites. These emissaries came disguised with old garments, old shoes, and provisions that appeared to be the remnants of a long journey. Upon meeting with Joshua, these ambassadors lied, stating they were from a far country but that word of Israel and Israel's God had reached them. The Gibeonites sought to make a covenant treaty with the Israelites. Joshua and the others were fooled by their appearance and made a grave error. Rather than asking for the Lord's direction, they proceeded to enter into a covenant with the Gibeonites (see Joshua 9:14).

Later, Joshua and the Israelites learned the truth. They were angry at having been duped and were left in a dilemma. Should they honor God's prior command to destroy all the inhabitants of the land, or should they honor their covenant, even though it had been entered into under false pretenses? The Israelites honored the covenant and refrained from destroying Gibeon, opting to make them servants instead. The Lord supported them in their decision.

And as if that weren't trying enough for the Israelites, it got worse. Once word spread of the covenant between Gibeon and Israel, some of the neighboring kingdoms banded together in a war against Gibeon. Now, not only did Israel have to refrain from destroying Gibeon but also were called upon to defend her as a covenant partner. Once again, Israel honored the covenant. And the Lord Himself went to battle with the Israelites against Gibeon's enemies. In fact, the scriptures record that the Lord cast down "great stones" from heaven and slew more of them than did the children of Israel (see Joshua 10:11).

Following this battle, Israel kept their covenant with Gibeon from generation to generation for about five hundred years. Eventually, overzealous King Saul broke it by slaying some of the Gibeonites. The Lord punished Israel for this offense by sending a famine that lasted three years. King David inquired and was told the famine was a result of Saul breaking the covenant with Gibeon. David made restitution by delivering, as demanded by the Gibeonites, seven of Saul's sons into their hands for hanging. King David spared Mephibosheth of this fate, for the sake of his oath with Jonathan (see 2 Samuel 21:1–7).

When we realize that these events occurred half a millennium later and with people who had nothing to do with the original covenant (that had been entered into under false pretenses), it serves as another powerful example of how seriously the Lord views covenants.

With this in mind, let us return to the Kirtland dedicatory prayer. In the same verse reminding us that God keeps covenants perfectly, we find some hope for ourselves: "and showest mercy unto thy servants who walk uprightly before thee, with all their hearts" (D&C 109:1). God recognizes that we do not keep our covenants perfectly all of the time. He shows mercy unto us, but in return He expects us to walk uprightly with all our hearts.

His claim that He "showest mercy" is, I believe, humbly under-stated. He is full of long-suffering. The allegory of Zenos (see Jacob 5) is a witness of the Lord's patience and long-suffering with the house of Israel. Israel's entire history and status as a covenant people is testimony, not to their greatness or faithfulness or their favored status (they often failed and should serve as a warning to us), but rather to how fully God intends to fulfill His covenants.

He tries over and over again until he finally asks three times, "What could I have done more for my vineyard?" (Jacob 5:41, 47, 49). Jacob concluded his recital of the allegory by admonishing us to repent and come unto God with full purpose of heart and to "cleave unto God as he cleaveth unto you" (Jacob 6:5).

Notice the similarity in the opening of the Kirtland dedicatory prayer with the dedication of Solomon's temple anciently: "And Sol-omon stood before the altar of the Lord in the presence of all the congregation of Israel, and spread forth his hands toward heaven: And he said, Lord God of Israel, there is no God like thee, in heaven above, or on earth beneath, *who keepest covenant and mercy with thy servants that walk before thee with all their heart*: Who hast kept with thy servant David my father that thou promisedst him" (1 Kings 8:22–24; emphasis added; see also D&C 109:1).

Solomon acknowledged that the Lord kept His promises to his father, David. The scriptures contain example after example of the Lord's promises fulfilled.[45] Truly, He is the same yesterday, today, and forever (see Mormon 9:9). And truly, He keeps His covenants perfectly. Of this we can have absolute faith and assurance.

Understanding the symbolism and meaning that covenants held anciently provides us with insight into and greater appreciation for our own gospel covenants. We gain a sense of the kind of relation-ship God wants to have with each of us, all of which attests to the greatness of God and His love and condescension toward His chil-dren. It's not about us being chosen or special. It's about God's great-ness and willingness to rescue us.

These blessings are available to all, but it remains up to us to enter into and then strive to keep our end of our covenants. We need to establish with the Lord the type of relationship and oneness implied in the covenant. This relationship is not automatic, it is but something we should work for. Let us avoid the mistake of being lifted up in pride like ancient Israel. Rather, let us seek to do the works of Abraham.

Homework

1. How is your relationship with your Savior and Heavenly Father? What could you do to "draw near" unto Him so that He can "draw near" unto you (see D&C 88:63)? How often do you have His Spirit in your life? Is He leading your path, and are you doing His will? Find some time to ponder these things.

2. When you have finished this book, you may want to return to this chapter and study the scriptural references on covenants contained within. The scriptures have a lot to say about covenants.

3. The doctrine of Christ is outlined three times in the Book of Mormon (2 Nephi 31–32; 3 Nephi 11; 27). What covenant is formed by this doctrine?

4. The sermon at the temple (comprising 3 Nephi 12–14) established the new covenant terms between Christ and His followers. What blessings, penalties and obligations do you find? How does this sermon relate to the temple endowment?[46] These teachings are the heart of the law of the gospel. Of all the things the Savior could have taught, following his Atonement, Resurrection and Ascension, He chose to give these teachings to the Nephites. What does that tell us of their importance?

5. In this chapter, we discussed covenants from a more personal, individual perspective. Recognize, though, that from the Lord's perspective, covenants influence and govern history as well. As you read the scriptures, what promises has the Lord made to Adam, Noah, Enoch, Lehi, Nephi, Enos, and others by covenant, which are being fulfilled in our day, or are yet to be fulfilled in the future?

CHAPTER 2

Gospel Ordinances

"Being born again, comes by the Spirit of God through ordinances."[47]

—Joseph Smith

What exactly are ordinances, and what purpose do they serve? To an outsider viewing them from a distance, ordinances can seem strange. Why are they even a part of the Lord's gospel, in ancient times and in our dispensation?

An ordinance is a religious ceremony or rite.[48] Ordinances are one means by which we enter into covenants with the Lord. They often mark important stages in our growth and changes in our relationship with the Lord. They are necessary. Joseph Smith taught, "The question is frequently asked, 'Can we not be saved without going through with all those ordinances, etc.?' I would answer, No, not the fulness of salvation."[49]

What is it about ordinances that is so important? We find a clue to this question in the First Vision. When Joseph entered the Sacred Grove and asked which of all the churches he should join, he learned that one of the problems in Christianity as a whole was that it had a form of godliness but denied the power thereof (see Joseph Smith—History

1:19). One of the things the Restoration needed to address was this lack of power. Later in his ministry, Joseph received a revelation informing us that "in the ordinances thereof, the *power of godliness* is manifest. And without the ordinances thereof, and the authority of the priesthood, the power of godliness is not manifest unto men in the flesh" (D&C 84:20–21, emphasis added). To once again make the "power of godliness" available, valid ordinances had to be restored.

In the Articles of Faith, we read, "We believe that through the Atonement of Christ, all mankind may be saved, by obedience to the laws and ordinances of the Gospel" (Articles of Faith 1:3). According to this statement, for us to be saved, three things are necessary: the Atonement, laws, and ordinances. The need for the Atonement and for our obedience is easily understood, but it leaves us with an obvious problem. Our obedience is so imperfect. And as Lehi pointed out, the law condemns us all. "And by the law no flesh is justified; or, by the law men are cut off" (2 Nephi 2:5). We will never save ourselves by our obedience (see Alma 22:14).

Most of us keenly recognize and sense the gap between God's perfection and ourselves. As we begin to come unto Him, our appreciation of that vast gulf may become more acute, particularly as we earnestly strive to keep all of His commandments. We come to recognize our utter dependence upon the Atonement. Lehi continued, "Wherefore, redemption cometh in and through the Holy Messiah; for he is full of grace and truth" (2 Nephi 2:6). We all need access to the Atonement, but how is that made available?

Ordinances help bridge this vast gap. They are part of the means the Lord has established for the blessings of the Atonement to flow into our lives. They are crucial. We cannot be saved, in the fullest sense of that word, without them (see John 3:5; Mark 16:16; 1 Peter 3:21; 3 Nephi 11:33). They allow the *power of godliness* begin to manifest itself in our lives. They can bring about our spiritual rebirth.

Most saving gospel ordinances have at least two primary purposes: to bring the blessings of the Atonement into our lives and to invite and prepare us to return to the Lord's presence.

However, simply receiving the ordinances is not enough. They are given conditionally. Receiving the full blessings they entail requires us to strive to live the covenants associated with them. Doing so will help us reach the point where we can truly offer up a broken heart and a contrite spirit (see 2 Nephi 2:7).

It is through gospel covenants received by ordinances that we are spiritually begotten of Christ, becoming His sons and His daughters, and eventually being sealed as His (see Mosiah 5:7, 15). Our only other choice is to procrastinate our repentance until the devil seals us as his (see Alma 34:35).

Jacob testified, along with his father, Lehi, that were it not for the Atonement, everyone would be lost and inevitably become angels to the devil (see 2 Nephi 9:8–9). That is our awful predicament. We are all fallen and lost. Christ is our only hope. Gospel ordinances and the associated covenants are a lifeline of grace thrown to us.

Returning to the Articles of Faith, number four states: "We believe that the *first principles and ordinances* of the Gospel are: first, Faith in the Lord Jesus Christ; second, Repentance; third, Baptism by immersion for the remission of sins; fourth, Laying on of hands for the gift of the Holy Ghost" (Articles of Faith 1:4; emphasis added). We might well ask in what sense are these principles and ordinances first? It is not that we can simply check them off of some list and move onto other things; rather, they form the basics, the foundation to which we should return to over and over and over again.

However, the fact that there are *first* ordinances suggests that there are also additional ones, which are likewise necessary. "All men who become heirs of God and joint heirs with Jesus Christ will have to receive the *fulness of the ordinances of his kingdom*; and those who will not receive *all the ordinances* will come short of the fulness of that glory, if they do not lose the whole."[50] These subsequent gospel ordinances, which include our temple ordinances, build upon and strengthen the foundation laid by the first ordinances. They are related to enduring to the end. The first ordinances are to bring about a spiritual rebirth. The additional ones serve to bring about spiritual growth and maturity.

Three Elements of Gospel Ordinances

Most gospel ordinances contain the following three elements:

- A covenant: the covenant contains obligations along with blessings. Some blessings are received at the time the covenant is made; others are promised for the future.

- An external physical action: the ordinance involves some physical action as part of the covenant-making process. This action can be witnessed by others and demonstrates to the outside world an inner commitment on the part of the participant.
- Symbolic teaching: ordinances also involve symbolism, which is designed to teach and instruct. The greater our appreciation of the symbolism, the deeper our reverence for and understanding of the ordinance.

Think about baptism and the sacrament. You can readily see these three elements in them. We can also find them in the ordinances of the temple. We discussed covenants in the first chapter; before moving on, let us briefly review symbolism.

Symbolism

Consider for a moment the difference between a routine and a ritual. Both can be something we participate in often. Both may be repetitive. For example, you might have a daily routine in the morning as you rise from bed and prepare for your day. You probably go through it without much thought. If we aren't careful, we can likewise find ourselves participating in gospel ordinances, such as the sacrament, in the same thoughtless, routine manner.

A ritual, on the other hand, can hold deep meaning in our lives. We should participate in rituals purposefully and with understanding of the underlying intent the ritual portrays. As we come to appreciate the symbolism built into gospel ordinances and the underlying realities associated with those symbols, then participating in ordinances can move from a mere routine to a sacred ritual that we cherish.

So why does the Lord use symbols in the temple to teach us? What reasons can you think of?[51] Sometimes symbols can communicate more effectively than words. Consider the symbol of a heart, for example.

This symbol can represent a physical organ in our body, but more often it is associated with complex feelings such as love or courage. It can also be used to reflect the spiritual or moral core of a person.

By adding a jagged line to the symbol, we completely change its meaning. Now we have a broken heart. Most of us have experienced a broken heart, so this little drawing on a page might bring to our minds painful memories and emotions.

Add an arrow to the original heart, and the meaning is changed again, this time to represent romantic love. (I hope this symbol invokes happy, joyful memories.)

In all of this, we must not confuse or mistake the symbol with the thing symbolized. If we only see the *hearts* in our examples above and miss the realities of courage, love, romance, or heartache that are represented, then we have missed the purpose of the symbol.

If we attend the temple and only see the *hearts*, we have missed the message. Elder John A. Widtsoe taught, "We live in a world of symbols. No man or woman can come out of the temple endowed as he [or she] should be, unless he has seen, beyond the symbol, the mighty realities for which the symbols stand."[52]

Despite the many differences in the circumstances of our individual lives, we share much in common. Symbols capture these commonalities, while still allowing for our individual experiences, interpretation, and adaption. By using symbols, the Lord makes the temple both universal and personal to each of His children.

May I suggest a few principles that may be helpful as you seek to understand the symbols of the temple. First, recognize that many symbols teach us of the Savior. "And behold, all things have their likeness, and all things are created and made to bear record of me, both things which are temporal, and things which are spiritual" (Moses 6:63). This is especially true in His house. As you encounter symbols in the temple, ask yourself what they teach you about Christ, His condescension and sacrifice, and your relationship with Him.

Second, symbols present an opportunity to learn. Whenever you encounter symbolism, whether it is found in the scriptures or in the temple, there exists an invitation to receive more knowledge through revelation. The Lord took the trouble to encode these things, and the Spirit can help you decode them.

Third, don't limit the Lord's use of symbols. One mistake I made for many years was thinking in terms of X and Y, or that X symbol must equal Y thing (X = Y). I failed to recognize that most temple symbols are multi-faceted and contain layer upon layer of meaning. Often, it would be more accurate to say X = Y as well as Z and A and B and D and Q and S.

For example, the mirrors in the sealing rooms reflect images that seem to extend on and on forever. Standing in between those mirrors and looking in both directions, you might see represented your past actions and the decisions that brought you to this point, your life at this moment in time, and your future course; or your ancestors and the generations preceding you, your life, and looking in the other direction, your posterity or the generations that will follow; or the premortal, mortal, and postmortal realms, which include all eternity to all eternity; or that your sealing, though given conditionally, is intended to last forever; or you might notice a slight curve as the images extend out, suggesting the course the Lord walks is one eternal round, which might also remind you that He is no respecter of persons and that He is as willing to bless *you* with the fulness of his gospel as He is any of His other children.

A great example of the Lord's use of symbolism is found in the vision of Lehi.[53] The vision comprises one chapter in the Book of Mormon and is filled with simple, day-to-day symbols (see 1 Nephi 8). Lehi interpreted these symbols as they related to his family. We often do likewise and apply them to our own spiritual journey through life. Lehi didn't explain everything, however, and Nephi asked for and was given an explanation of the symbols. Nephi's vision covers four chapters (see 1 Nephi 11–14). And yet Nephi testified that he saw the same things his father saw (see 1 Nephi 11:3; 14:29). The explanation of these same symbols to Nephi included the Savior's birth, life, and ministry; the Twelve Apostles; the land of promise and its inhabitants; the Savior's visit to the Americas; and much of the history of the world, including the founding of America; the Restoration of the gospel; and the winding-up scenes before the Second Coming. All of this information was also contained in the symbols of Lehi's dream. In the temple endowment presentation, we are given a simplified "Lehi" version. But the expanded "Nephi" version is there as well. For us to see it will require us to ask the Lord for help, as did Nephi.

Fourth, let the Lord be your teacher. One day, I went to the temple confused about an aspect of the endowment and sincerely wanted to understand it better. I know a brother—let us call him Brother Jones. Brother Jones is retired and chooses to attend the temple daily. He does three endowment sessions each day, from Tuesday through Friday, and works in the baptistry on Saturday mornings. My plan was to wait in the celestial room until Brother Jones arrived, and then to ask him my question. I figured if anyone would know the answer, Brother Jones would. I knew which session he would be attending and when he would be out.

As I sat in the celestial room waiting for Brother Jones to arrive, I began to pray. As I prayed, the Lord told me, "Don't trouble Brother Jones. I will teach you." As much as I wanted an answer that day, I decided to trust the Lord and left without seeing Brother Jones. And over the next year and a half, the Lord did teach me. I'm convinced that the things He taught me I could not have received from Brother Jones. It is good to gain an understanding of scriptural symbols.[54] This book is intended to provide some basics. But in the end, let the Lord teach you.

In the remainder of this book, we will discuss general aspects of the temple that I believe apply to us all. Again, take what feels right and helpful to you and discard anything that does not. Your understanding of a particular symbol may be different from mine, and both may be correct.

Homework

1. Ponder this week on the symbolism in the sacrament and what it means to you. Is this ordinance something more than renewing your baptismal covenant? How are the three elements present in this ordinance?

2. You should acquire a basic literacy in the language of symbolism. A helpful introduction to some common symbols is found at www.ldssymbols.com. Another reference is Alonzo Gaskill's book *The Lost Language of Symbolism: An Essential Guide for Recognizing and Interpreting Symbols of the Gospel* (Salt Lake City: Desert Book, 2003). You may find these helpful. However, neither of these sources are comprehensive. Nor do I believe we should limit the Lord's use of any of these symbols. There are generally additional meanings associated with all of these symbols, as Nephi's experience highlights.

CHAPTER 3

Initiatory

"Whereby are given unto us exceeding great and precious promises: that by these ye might be partakers of the divine nature."

—2 Peter 1:4

I n the previous chapter, we established that there are additional gospel ordinances beyond baptism, which are also necessary. These include the ordinances of the temple. While the specifics of temple ordinances are sacred, what those ordinances are is not a secret. A recent general conference address listed them as "initiatory ordinances, endowments, marriages, sealings, baptisms for the dead, and ordinations."[55] Over the next several chapters, we will cover some background and context to assist us in better understanding these temple ordinances.

Your temple endowment begins with the initiatory ordinances. The word *initiatory* is derived from the word *initiate*. One meaning of the word is "to cause a process or action to begin." If we apply this definition to the temple's initiatory ordinances, the question naturally arises: What are we beginning?

President David O. McKay answered, "I believe there are few, even temple workers, who comprehend the full meaning and power of the temple endowment. *Seen for what it is, it is the step-by-step ascent into the Eternal Presence. If our young people could only glimpse it, it would be the most powerful spiritual motivation of their lives.*"[56] In the following chapters, we will try to gain such a glimpse.

The Church's booklet *Preparing to Enter the Holy Temple* defines the initiatory ordinances as washing, anointing, and being clothed in the garments. It further states that "associated with the endowment are washings and anointings—mostly symbolic in nature, but promising definite, immediate blessings as well as future blessings. In connection with these ordinances, in the temple you will be officially clothed in the garment and promised marvelous blessings in connection with it."[57] In part, this quote is included here to ease concerns some readers may have with listing the washing, anointing, and clothing as parts of the initiatory.

Beyond this brief description, the scriptures shed additional light on our own ordinances. In Exodus, we read: "And thou shalt bring Aaron and his sons unto the door of the tabernacle of the congregation, and wash them with water. And thou shalt put upon Aaron the holy garments, and anoint him, and sanctify him; that he may minister unto me in the priest's office" (Exodus 40:12–13). This scripture provides a where, a what, a why, and a who for these ordinances. Let us examine each of these for a moment.

The Where of the Initiatory Ordinances

Moses was instructed that these ordinances were to be performed in a specific location. Why would that be significant? Why did they need to be done at the door of the tabernacle of the congregation?

Moses's tabernacle had three main areas. (Refer to the following illustration.) These three areas corresponded with increasing levels of holiness.

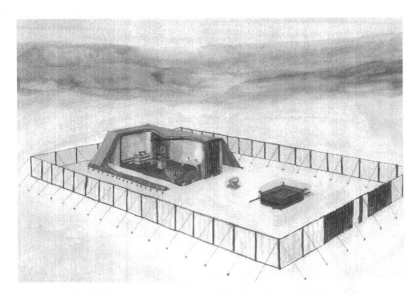

First, the Outer Court. The Outer Court was the largest of the three spaces. It was where the sacrifices took place, where the altar was located, and where vessels for washing were found. The priests and the Israelite congregation mingled here in performing and participating in rites. This area symbolized the telestial kingdom.

Next, the Holy Place. This is the space located immediately inside the inner tent, or the temple building. It contained the table for shewbread (the bread of life), an altar of incense (the smoke rising from this incense represented Israel's prayers ascending heavenward), and the Menorah (a seven branched candlestick representing the tree of life). Into this area, the priests alone entered twice a day, in the morning and again in the evening. Here they burned incense, lit the candles, and replaced the shewbread. This area represented the terrestrial kingdom.

Third, the Holy of Holies. This area was the smallest of the three and formed a cube. It was considered the most sacred or holy spot in Judaism. It housed the ark of the covenant with the Ten Commandments. The ark represented not only the covenant between God and Israel, but also the throne of God and His presence in Israel. Into this place, only the high priest was permitted to enter, and then only once a year for a specific set of ordinances on the Day of Atonement. This space symbolized the celestial kingdom.

The washing, anointing, and clothing ordinances administered by Moses prepared Aaron's sons to enter the Holy Place (terrestrial realm) as priests and fitted Aaron as the high priest to cross the veil into the Holy of Holies (celestial realm), where the throne of God was found. God had promised to meet with His people there (see Exodus 29:43).

Recognize that one purpose of these ordinances was to prepare for entering sacred space. They took place at the door of the tabernacle prior to Aaron and his sons entering holier places. Our initiatory ordinances serve the same purpose.

The What of the Initiatory Ordinances

Moses was instructed to wash, anoint, and clothe Aaron and his sons, which brings up a question: Why washing with water? One obvious response is because no unclean thing can be admitted into the presence of the Lord (see Moses 6:57; 1 Nephi 10:21). But is there more to it than that?

We live in a fallen, unclean world. We are washed at the onset of our endowment. But in the sequence of gospel ordinances, this washing occurs after our baptism. Is it done to clean up anything amiss since baptism? Or is there another purpose? In our work for the dead, they are washed right after being baptized and confirmed. So there must be some purpose in the washing beyond what is received through baptism.

In part, the answer to this question is given in the preface of the ordinance. Go to the temple. Perform some initiatory ordinances and listen to the purpose as explained there. The initiatory ordinances continue the symbolism of spiritual rebirth that was commenced by baptism, but baptism is an ordinance of justification while the initiatory washing and anointing is one of sanctification.

As part of the initiatory ordinances, you are given specific blessings. Those blessings are physical, spiritual, and symbolic in nature. Ponder on what they mean and how they apply to your life. In them, you are promised the help you need to succeed in your life's mission. Before a big event or decision in your life, you might seek a father's blessing. My children ask for one each year before beginning a new year at school. In one simple sense, the initiatory ordinances are a little like returning home and receiving a father's blessing from Heavenly Father.

On the day you were endowed, you left the temple with sacred promises given directly to you. Not promises made to some ancient prophet. Not promises made to some other person. Promises made to you. If you are faithful, the fulfillment of those promises is sufficient to see you through all that you were foreordained and sent here to do. As part of your endowment, you are given every blessing you need to succeed in your life and in your journey back to God.

After washing, Moses was to also anoint and sanctify Aaron. To *anoint* means to smear or rub with oil as part of a sacred rite. Anointing was part of the ceremonial conferral of a divine or holy office upon a priest or a king (see 1 Samuel 16:13; 1 Kings 1:39). To *sanctify* means to make holy, set apart for a holy purpose, or consecrate to the service of God.

We are anointed with olive oil. Olive oil is a symbol of the Holy Ghost and its influence. It is associated with sanctification, revelation, consecration, healing, and the Atonement. In the Church, we speak often of the Holy Ghost as the Comforter, but one of its primary purposes is to sanctify us (see 3 Nephi 27:19–20). As part of your initiatory, you are symbolically anointed from head to toe with the Holy Ghost.

Furthermore, how might your temple anointing be related to the plea found in the dedicatory prayer of the Kirtland Temple, that we might grow up in the Lord and receive a fulness of the Holy Ghost (see D&C 109:15)? What does it mean to receive a fulness of the Holy Ghost? Is being anointed with the symbol (olive oil) the same thing as actually receiving a fulness of the Holy Ghost? Or is the anointing a promise requiring a future fulfillment?

Consider how this scripture might also apply to our discussion: "God anointed Jesus of Nazareth with the Holy Ghost and with power: who went about doing good, and healing all that were oppressed of the devil; for God was with him" (Acts 10:38). One of Christ's titles, *the Messiah*, literally means "the Anointed."

In the Old Testament, we find three groups who were anointed: prophets (see, for example, 1 Kings 19:16), priests (see Exodus 29:7–9), and kings (see 1 Samuel 16:13–14). Those anointed were *meshiah*, meaning "anointed one." These anointed ones could be properly referred to as *messiahs*, and their lives were to be a type or reflection of the Messiah. So likewise, as we are anointed, our lives should also reflect His. He should be able to work through us to bless others.

Exodus does not tell us specifically how Aaron's washing and anointing were performed; however, we are given more detail as to his consecration. We read, "And he slew it [the ram]; and Moses took of the blood of it, and put it upon the tip of Aaron's right ear, and upon the thumb of his right hand, and upon the great toe of his right foot" (Leviticus 8:23).

Now, if you haven't been endowed and are reading this, rest assured that there is no blood used in our modern temples. But what is really going on in this scripture with Aaron? It is describing Aaron being set apart (consecrated) for his priesthood service. The blood of the ram, representing the blood (the sacrifice and the Atonement) of our Savior, is smeared on his ear, thumb, and big toe.

Why was this blood put on Aaron's ear? Think about what the ear represents. Ears symbolize that which we chose to listen to and obey. We are constantly bombarded with competing messages. Which voices should we hearken to? This act of smearing blood suggests that Aaron's ear needed to be closely tuned into his Lord's voice and reminded him of his constant need to hear the Lord's word.

In our own lives, it might be good to reflect on how our relationship is with the Savior. How often do we hear His voice? How might we increase our ability to discern and listen to Him? Our ears should also be attuned to Him.

After his ear, blood was next placed upon Aaron's thumb and then on his big toe. Again, think about what the thumb, or hand, represents. Our hands are related to our actions and what we choose to do. The toe or foot is symbolic of our daily walk, our path through life, and the goals we pursue.

This ordinance symbolically taught Aaron how closely he needed to be to his Savior. It was a reminder to hearken to the Savior and hear His words. It also suggested that all of his actions and his path through life should follow the Lord. But there is more. The symbol goes both ways. It also represents a promise that the Lord will speak to Aaron's ear, that He will strengthen Aaron's hands, and that He will walk by Aaron through his days. His Atonement would in turn cover Aaron's choices, actions, and path through life.

What about the promises given in the temple initiatory? Have you reflected on what they mean to you in your daily life? Are those promises literal or symbolic? Physical or spiritual? Applicable to this life or preparation for the resurrection? If you have not had the opportunity recently, try to return to the temple soon and participate in the initiatory ordinances to review your promises. Memorize them if you are able and ponder on what they mean in your life.

The first time I participated in the initiatory ordinances for proxy names was about ten years after my mission. Though I had frequently attended the temple with my wife, we generally ended up in endowment sessions or sometimes participated in sealings. It never really occurred to us to do initiatory work. I'm not sure what prompted me on that particular day. But as the officiator began, the Spirit enveloped and filled me. It was impressed upon me how sacred these ordinances are, along with their associated blessings. It was one of the spiritual highlights of my life, and the spirit of that day lingered through the week that followed.

Many of the promises given are symbolic. As an example, consider a promise from the Word of Wisdom. We are told that if we keep it, we shall run and not be weary and walk and not faint (see D&C 89:20). I have faithfully kept the Word of Wisdom throughout my life, yet if I run a few miles, I am rather weary. And if I tried to run an entire marathon, I'd probably faint. So what is really being promised here?

This promise is related to our ability to endure to the end and run, with patience, the race through life set before us. Like Paul, we will be able to say, "I have fought a good fight, I have finished my course, I have kept the faith: henceforth there is laid up for me a crown of righteousness, which the Lord, the righteous judge, shall give me at that day: and not to me only, but unto all them also that love his appearing" (2 Timothy 4:7–8). Ask the Lord to help you understand the promises you've received and how they are being fulfilled in your life.

Finally, as part of these preparatory ordinances, Aaron and his sons were clothed in sacred ceremonial clothing. This clothing was designed to teach and testify about God and His relationship with them. It held symbolic meaning. As part of our endowment, we too are clothed in holy garments. Why is that even necessary, and what does it symbolize for us?

When Adam and Eve discovered they were naked, they tried to hide from the Lord. They didn't want to be in His presence in their nakedness. God clothed them to remedy the situation (see Genesis 3:21). This clothing wasn't simply about covering a nude body. Their real nakedness was their guilt, fallen nature, weaknesses and sins, frailties and vulnerabilities, and the loss of their prior glory as they descended into mortality. The garment, made by God and fashioned through sacrifice, was to cover their lost and fallen condition. It is the same for us.

Jacob, speaking of the afterlife, taught his people that "we shall have a perfect knowledge of all our guilt, and our uncleanness, and our nakedness; and the righteous shall have a perfect knowledge of their enjoyment, and their righteousness, being clothed with purity, yea, even with the robe of righteousness" (2 Nephi 9:14). Notice the difference between the two conditions described. It is the presence or absence of holy garments.

After this life, we can probably suppose everyone would want to go to heaven to live with God. This seems natural because we know that God loves us. So much so, in fact, that John stated "God is love" (1 John 4:8). And we know that God loved the world so much He sent His Son here to save us (see John 3:17). So why is it that prophets or others who encounter God or heavenly messengers often feel fear as their first reaction?[58] That seems odd. God loves us with an infinite love. And yet our reaction at His coming into the presence of pure love is fear. Why?

Moroni, who had been in the Lord's presence, warned, "For behold, when ye shall be brought to see your *nakedness* before God, and also the glory of God, and the holiness of Jesus Christ, *it will kindle a flame of unquenchable fire upon you*" (Mormon 9:5; emphasis added). King Benjamin gave the same warning, which he received from an angel: "Therefore if that man repenteth not, and remaineth and dieth an enemy to God, the demands of divine justice do awaken his immortal soul to a lively sense of his own guilt, which doth cause him to shrink from the presence of the Lord, and doth fill his breast with guilt, and pain, and anguish, which is like an unquenchable fire, whose flame ascendeth up forever and ever" (Mosiah 2:38).

Moroni continued, "Do ye suppose that ye could be happy to dwell with that holy Being, when your souls are racked with a consciousness of guilt that ye have ever abused his laws? Behold, I say unto you that ye would be more miserable to dwell with a holy and just God, under a consciousness of your filthiness before him, than ye would to dwell with the damned souls in hell" (Mormon 9:3–4). Think about that for a moment. If we are not prepared to return to God's presence, we would be more comfortable in *hell* than with Him.

It's easy to think of ourselves as being righteous and apply these scriptures to the wicked, especially if we are living the standards of the Church when others are not. It's so easy to think, *Surely, I'm not naked. It must be those other people.*

Perhaps we should be more careful in our confidence of our own worthiness when measured from God's perspective. Remember, these ancient prophets stood in the Lord's presence. We look to them as examples and consider them righteous. Yet even their initial reaction in encountering heavenly glory was fear.

The fear came from seeing and understanding the great gulf between themselves and the holiness of God, in whose presence they stood. As good as their lives may have been by our standards, when measured against absolute purity and holiness, they felt completely inadequate. Isaiah states that we are all unclean things, and all our righteousness is as filthy rags (see Isaiah 64:6). Moses exclaimed, after his encounter with God, "Now . . . I know that man is nothing" (Moses 1:10). It is easy to see why the Book of Mormon warns us that "this life is the time for men to prepare to meet God" (Alma 34:32).

No wonder Adam and Eve, upon discovering their nakedness, sought to hide from the Lord. Because of the Fall, we find ourselves in the same condition. Like Adam and Eve, we need to be clothed by the Lord to cover our nakedness. Sadly, some will not ever recognize their nakedness until the moment when they have returned to God's presence. Then it will be painfully apparent.

Along with the temple garment that clothes us, we are promised protection. This protection is not simply an extra layer of cotton-poly fabric, nor is it "magic underwear," as it is sometimes portrayed. So what does this promise really mean?

To answer this, consider what the garment symbolizes. Remember our discussion on covenantal marks. The Savior carries covenantal marks in His flesh. We also bear covenantal marks, not in our flesh, but nevertheless upon our person as we wear our garments. In the Nauvoo Temple, these marks were cut into the garment rather than sewn in. This was done at the end of the endowment in front of the veil.[59] There is a connection between the temple veil and your individual garments.

Prior to the Savior's Atonement, only the high priest could enter the Holy of Holies in the temple or tabernacle, and then only under specific conditions and for specific purposes (see Leviticus 16). The temple veil represented, among other things, a barrier between God and His people. At the moment of the Savior's death, this veil was torn in two from top to bottom (see Matthew 27:51). Through His sacrifice, the Savior opened a way for men to return to the Lord's presence. The barrier was overcome.

Speaking of these things, Paul said, "Having therefore, brethren, boldness to enter into the holiest [the Holy of Holies or the presence of God] by the blood of Jesus, by a new and living way, which he hath consecrated for us, through *the veil, that is to say, his flesh*" (Hebrews 10:19–20; emphasis added). Here, Paul tied the symbolism of the veil to the flesh of Christ. It was Christ's sacrifice that opened the way.

Individual garments symbolize a number of things, including your covenants, the veil of the temple, and the Atonement. But they also symbolize Christ and the marks of His covenant. When you dress in the morning and put on your garments, you are symbolically taking Christ upon you. The protection promised comes not from an extra layer of fabric, but from Him. Once that is understood why would anyone ever remove his or her garments unnecessarily?

The Why of the Initiatory Ordinances

Returning to Exodus, let's consider the *why* of these ordinances. Why are they important? One answer is given at the end of the verse: "And thou shalt bring Aaron and his sons unto the door of the tabernacle of the congregation, and wash them with water. And thou shalt put upon Aaron the holy garments, and anoint him, and sanctify him; *that he may minister unto me in the priest's office*" (Exodus 40:12–13, emphasis added). All of this was done to prepare Aaron for his ministry.

Missionaries are endowed prior to leaving on their missions for the same reason: to prepare them for their ministry. A new couple entering into marriage and raising a family is likewise beginning a lifelong ministry. This is one reason why brothers and sisters, if not previously endowed, are endowed before their weddings.

In the dedicatory prayer of the Kirtland Temple (see D&C 109), we learn a great deal about the Lord's purposes for His house. Remember that at this point in the history of the Church, only the initiatory ordinances had been given to the Saints. With that in mind, consider this plea: "And we ask thee, Holy Father, that *thy servants may go forth from this house armed with thy power*, and that *thy name may be upon them*, and *thy glory be round about them*, and *thine angels have charge over them*; and from this place they may bear exceedingly great and glorious tidings, in truth, unto the ends of the earth, that they may know that this is thy work, and that thou hast put forth thy hand, to fulfil that which thou hast spoken by the mouths of the prophets, concerning the last days" (D&C 109:22–23; emphasis added). We need these blessings to succeed in our own ministries. You need to be armed with God's power and have His name upon you, His glory round about you, and His angels with you. And, if you will live for them, you received these promises in your initiatory. These blessings give us a sense of how sacred these ordinances are and how personal they should be.

In summary, we've considered several purposes for the initiatory ordinances. These include the following.

- To prepare us to enter sacred space
- To cover our nakedness
- To sanctify us and make us holy
- To bless and prepare us for our ministry
- To strengthen and endow us with all we need to accomplish our mission and purpose in life
- To invite us to grow up in the Lord and receive a fulness of the Holy Ghost
- To prepare us to return to God

Beyond these seven, there are yet other purposes. One of which is to extend an invitation or calling. Let's consider that next.

An Initiate

As a noun, the word *initiate* refers to someone who has been initiated, or introduced (usually by a ritual), into a select society or group. Could this definition also apply to our ordinances? And if so, what group or society might it be referring to? Once again, we find clues in the scriptures. John, speaking of Christ, recorded that He "loved us, and washed us from our sins in his own blood, and hath made us kings and priests unto God" (Revelation 1:5–6). One of Christ's titles is King of Kings and Lord of Lords (see Revelation 17:14). To *kings and priests*, we would add *queens and priestesses* for the women.

This raises the question: Does a society or group of kings and queens, priests and priestesses exist? Yes, though the scriptures refer to it as the Church of the Firstborn (see D&C 76:54). "They are they into whose hands the Father has given all things—They are they who are priests and kings, who have received of his fulness, and of his glory" (D&C 76:55–56). Becoming a member of this group is clearly something much greater than what we receive in the initiatory ordinances. But your invitation to rise up and join this group is found within the initiatory ordinances.

Speaking to a group of young missionaries about to receive their endowments, President David O. McKay encouraged them to look beyond the simple mechanics of the ordinances and see the glorious meaning and purpose behind them. He admonished, "Let your spiritual eyes see the significance of that anointing, and then you will realize what it means to be initiated into the House of God." He then explained, you are "anointed to become a king and priest of the Most High; a queen and priestess in the realms of God. Now that is what it means. I do not know how long it will take you or me to achieve that, but we are anointed that we may become such."[60]

You receive this calling in the initiatory. It is given conditionally upon your subsequent faithfulness. Actually receiving these blessings will depend upon you. Unfortunately, some will not succeed. We are warned that while many are called, few are chosen (see D&C 121:34). And the reasons for the many failures are given; one is that our hearts are set too much upon the things of this world and the honors of men (see D&C 121:35).

We tend to think of these blessings in terms of the next life. And they may sound pretty good to us. After all, when you are a king or queen, everyone has to do what you say, right? But think about what these things potentially mean in this life.

Consider Nephi's example as a king and priest. As a *king*, Nephi served his people's temporal needs. He helped provide for them. He taught his people how to build buildings and how to work with wood and metal (see 2 Nephi 5:15). He defended them in war (see 2 Nephi 5:14; Jacob 1:10). Nephi didn't seek to be a king (see 2 Nephi 5:18); it wasn't what he wanted. And he wasn't a king as we picture kings. He was a servant-king like King Benjamin and King Mosiah, who, like their Lord, knelt to serve (2 Nephi 6:2).

Nephi's people were his family and his extended family, and he labored all his days for their welfare (see Jacob 1:10). He prayed for them, suffered for and with them, and sought their well-being continually (see 2 Nephi 33:3). His record and ministry as a king and the history of his people were recorded on his large plates (see 2 Nephi 5:33).

How different this is from many of the examples of leaders in our modern world. Christ warned that men will seek power, dominion, and to exercise authority over others, but we should rather seek to minister and serve (see Matthew 20:25–28). Christ Himself came to minister. Nephi, like His master, sought to do the same.

In a more recent example from the history of the United States, consider the vast difference between President George Washington—who sacrificed so much of his personal fortune and suffered alongside his men through terrible hardships to purchase our freedoms, and who also refused to be a king—with some politicians and world leaders today. On the one hand, we find a true servant-leader. On the other, we see those who seek power, dominion, and authority; who are filled with pride; and who live extravagant lifestyles while others around them suffer.

And it is not just in politics. We find the same in sports, business, education, and even churches and charities. In any organization of people, there always seem to be those who seek to promote themselves at others' expense and are oblivious to the needs around them. No wonder the scriptures lament, "It is the nature and disposition of almost all men . . . to exercise unrighteous dominion" (D&C 121:39).

And as a result, "many are called, but few are chosen" (D&C 121:40). What a terrible price to pay. We need to wake up!

When my oldest son was serving as a missionary, I wrote him with the following advice:

> Don't get caught up in mission politics. Don't seek or campaign to become a district leader, zone leader, AP, or any other leadership position. Don't evaluate your mission experience based upon these things. Don't evaluate others based upon them either. Seek to serve God. Seek to serve his children. Serve wherever you are called and to the best of your ability. Don't turn away leadership roles if you are asked, but don't ever let them lift you up in pride. You serve. You follow Nephi's example throughout your life. Be wiser than I. So much of my life, I have gotten so many things wrong. My resolution this year is to repent and do better. I'd like to start getting them right.

As a *priest*, Nephi ministered to his people's spiritual needs. He taught them the scriptures and commandments. He built a temple and officiated in ordinances and ceremonies (see 2 Nephi 5:16). He consecrated Jacob and Joseph to be priests and teachers as well (see 2 Nephi 5:26). Again, in his role as a priest, Nephi didn't seek recognition or gain (which is priestcraft), but rather to serve, lift, and bless.

Finally, as a *prophet*, Nephi served his posterity and us. His ministry as a prophet is recorded on his small plates. His prophecy, testimony, vision, and warnings speak loudly and relevantly to our day. And Nephi testified that we are accountable for how we receive these things at the final judgment (see 2 Nephi 33:11, 15).

In the initiatory ordinances, you too are called to become a king and priest or a queen and priestess unto God. Recognize what that calling means for you here and now in this life. Go and serve, as did Nephi.

Homework

1. Return to the temple and participate in the initiatory ordinances. Memorize the blessings pronounced and ponder on their meanings in your life.

2. Some additional questions for you to consider:

- Are the promised blessings applicable to this life or the resurrection? Or both? How so?

- What does it mean to you to have promises made directly from God to *you*? Remember that "my word shall not pass away, but shall all be fulfilled" and that, in the case of these ordinances, "whether by mine own voice or by the voice of my servants, it is the same" (D&C 1:38).
- Are the initiatory blessings admonitions to you, or help promised to you?
- Why do these ordinances need to be received with a physical body? Couldn't they be received in the spirit world? Why does it need to happen here in mortality?
- Why are you washed after being baptized? What's the difference in the purposes of these two ordinances?

3. Read Doctrine and Covenants Section 109. This section contains the dedicatory prayer of the Kirtland Temple and was given by revelation. Remember that at this point in the Restoration, the only ordinances offered in the temple were similar to those in the initiatory. What does section 109 teach you of the Lord's purposes of temples and for these ordinances?

4. Peter testified, "According as his [Jesus Christ's] divine power hath given unto us all things that pertain unto life and godliness. . . . *Whereby are given unto us exceeding great and precious promises: that by these ye might be partakers of the divine nature,* having escaped the corruption that is in the world through lust" (2 Peter 1:3–4; emphasis added).

    How might this scripture relate to the temple ordinances? With this scripture in mind, you might wonder: What are the promises you've been given? Are they to help you partake of the divine nature? How and why does lust lead to corruption? What are the lusts we experience? Nephi identified them as lusts for power, popularity, riches, and flesh (see 1 Nephi 22:23).

    Peter continued, "And beside this, giving all diligence, add to your faith virtue; and to virtue knowledge; and to knowledge temperance; and to temperance patience; and to patience godliness; and to godliness brotherly kindness; and to brotherly kindness charity." This suggests a progression in these virtues. Are they interrelated? "For if these things be in you, and abound, they make you that ye shall neither be barren nor unfruitful in the knowledge of our Lord Jesus Christ" (2 Peter 1:5–8).

5. How might the following scriptures relate to the initiatory ordinances? Luke 1:69; Acts 10:38; 3 Nephi 27:19–20; 1 Samuel 16:13–14; D&C 76:40–42; Alma 5:57–58; Moses 6:59–60; 1 John 2:27; 2 Corinthians 1:21–22; Acts 26:18; Hebrews 13:12; 1 Peter 1:2; 2 Peter 1:4; Helaman 3:35; Moroni 10:33; D&C 20:29–32; 43:16; 84:20–21, 23.

CHAPTER 4

Your Endowment

And [Jacob] dreamed, and behold a ladder set up on the earth, and the top of it reached to heaven: and behold the angels of God ascending and descending on it. And, behold, the Lord stood above it, and said, I am the Lord God of Abraham thy father, and the God of Isaac. . . .

And, behold, I am with thee, and will keep thee in all places whither thou goest. . . .

And Jacob awaked out of his sleep, and he said, Surely the Lord is in this place; and I knew it not. . . .

This is none other but the house of God; and this is the gate of heaven. . . . And he called the name of that place Beth-el.

—Genesis 28:12–13, 15–17, 19

Some have left the temple after being endowed, feeling a little bit disappointed with their experience. President David O. McKay once shared his feelings:

Do you remember when you first went through the House of the Lord? I do. And I went out disappointed. Just a young man, out of college, anticipating great things when I went to the Temple. I was disappointed and grieved, and I have met hundreds of young men and young women since who had that experience. I have now found out why. There are two things in every Temple: mechanics, to set forth certain ideals, and symbolism, what those mechanics symbolize. I saw only the mechanics when I first went through the Temple. I did not see the spiritual. I did not see the symbolism of spirituality. . . . I was blind to the great lesson of purity behind the mechanics. I did not hear the message of the Lord. . . . How many of us young men saw that? We thought we were big enough and with intelligence sufficient to criticize the mechanics of it and we were blind to the symbolism, the message of the spirit. . . . The whole thing is simple in the mechanical part of it, but sublime and eternal in its significance.[61]

I was endowed in August 1985 in the Logan Utah Temple. On that summer afternoon, I entered the temple without a clue as to what to expect. The only preparation I received was from my father. As we crossed the parking lot walking up to the front door of the temple, he whispered to me, "Just remember, all the bows go on the same side." *What?! Gee, thanks, Dad! That sure eased my jitters.* His statement left me feeling apprehensive and confused, though I'm certain he meant well. What was I getting myself into? At the time, I did not know that the temple endowment involved ceremonial clothing. Later, of course, his advice proved helpful, and I still remember and think of it whenever I attend.

As I left the temple that day, I honestly did not understand what had just transpired. I remember feeling the Spirit to a greater extent than ever before in my life, but parts of the experience seemed kind of weird. It certainly wasn't anything like what I thought it might be or expected it to be. I sensed there was something deeply sacred about the temple, but I did not understand it.

You may have had similar feelings. If you haven't been and are preparing or planning to go, the best advice I can give you is to simply relax and enjoy the Spirit during your first time. Don't try to remember everything. There will be a guide and people to help you along the way, so just enjoy the wonderful outpouring of the Spirit. You can begin to learn and understand more little by little as you return.

A few years ago, while serving as a temple worker, I had the opportunity to help guide young men coming to the temple to receive their own ordinances. In nearly every case, they were ill prepared to understand the experience. It needn't be that way. Nor should there be so many good Saints who have served faithfully in the Church throughout their adult lives and yet still do not understand the temple. President McKay believed the endowment to be "one of the most beautiful things ever given to man," but he lamented that few people in the Church really comprehend it.[62] We need to change that; it is possible to gain understanding, here and now in this life.

Abraham reached a point in his life where he recognized there was more to the gospel than he possessed. He wanted to receive more. He described himself as one who had been a follower of righteousness. He desired to possess great knowledge and to be an even greater follower of righteousness (see Abraham 1:2). That should describe each of us as well. Do we recognize that there may be more to the gospel than we presently have? Abraham knew there was, so he sought for it.

Alma expressed a similar idea. He stated, "He that will harden his heart, the same receiveth the lesser portion of the word; and he that will not harden his heart, to him is given the greater portion of the word, until it is given unto him to know the mysteries of God until he know them in full" (Alma 12:10). Regardless of how much we have already learned, the endowment still seems to have more to offer.

So what exactly is our endowment? The word *endow* means to give the gift of an asset or an ability. The phrase *to endow*, from the Greek word *enduein,* means to dress, clothe, put on garments or attributes, or receive virtue. If our endowment is a gift, then we might ask what is the gift? How are we clothed? What virtue or attributes do we receive? To begin to answer these questions, let us break the endowment down into some of its component parts.

Covenants

In the temple endowment, we enter into a series of covenants with the Lord. There are five primary covenants we make. Pause for a moment and see if you can name all of them. If not, then next time you attend the temple, pay careful attention to learning them. We should know and understand what we have vowed to do.

The gospel contains many concepts that at first seem paradoxical. For example, the scriptures declare that man is nothing, even less than the dust of the earth (see Helaman 12:7)—and yet we are everything to God, whose work and glory is to bring about our immortality and eternal life (see Moses 1:39). On the surface, these truths seem contradictory. How can we be nothing and everything? Yet both are true. Like two sides to a coin, the full truth requires us to integrate both ideas.

We encounter a similar dilemma with respect to our covenants. Covenants are most sacred and serious. After reading the previous chapters, you likely have a sense of how the Lord feels about them. He will *never* violate a covenant He has made. God's words cannot return void; they must and will be fulfilled (see Moses 4:30). His word is the law upon which our universe operates. One of the great blessings of the temple ordinances is receiving God's words promised directly to us, conditional only upon our faithfulness.

Understanding this, we should not enter into covenants with God lightly or without intent to fulfill our part. These are not things to trifle with, and it is why we must be prepared before entering the temple and making covenants. The story of Ananias and Sapphira, who lied to Peter about the price of the property they sold and lost their lives as a result, may seem harsh until we realize they were under covenant and chose to deliberately and knowingly violate their covenant, thereby incurring the associated penalty (see Acts 5:1–11). God expects us to diligently strive to keep our covenants. And it is good for us to reflect upon how we are doing at living them.

Such reflection quickly points out the need for all of us to look at the other side of this coin. Fully living up to our covenants can seem daunting. After all, when we enter the temple for the first time and leave several hours later, we aren't magically transformed into a different person. We still face the same challenges, temptations, and struggles in our daily lives. Not one of us leaves the temple and fully keeps all of our covenants perfectly 100 percent of the time thereafter. The Lord understands this and gives us hope.

The gospel is intended to involve growth and progression. I believe the idea of learning and progressing is built into the wording of the covenants we make. We covenant to *observe and keep* certain laws and requirements rather than to simply *keep* such laws.[63] To *observe* implies a period of watching, learning, and growing as we increase in our ability to *keep* our covenants. It is a process that takes time.

If you think about that, it makes sense. One does not simply pick up a violin for the first time and play a beautiful melody. When the bow hits the strings in the hands of a beginner, the sound is grating and horrible. It takes hours of instruction and practice, followed by more instruction and still more practice to learn. Mastering it requires many years. Only then can a beautiful symphony be performed. The same is true with any worthwhile endeavor in life.

Is the gospel any different? Putting off the natural man, loving our neighbors, learning to hear and follow the Spirit, becoming more like Christ, and fully keeping our covenants requires instruction, diligent effort, and practice. It requires the best we can give, but the process will still be punctuated with mistakes along the way. We will hit many sour notes as we learn to play the gospel melody. Our mistakes shouldn't cause us to give up learning to play the violin, and neither should our errors and weaknesses prevent us from coming to Christ. Rather the opposite—they should bring us to Him.

The point is to get our hearts in the right place, and then go to work. As we do so, Christ covers our imperfections while we learn, grow, and develop. We do not enter the temple for the first time as beginners in this process of learning to live the gospel. We should already be dedicated disciples, but we also shouldn't feel we need to be perfect before coming to the temple.

The following statement by Elder Packer is comforting:

> When you come to the temple and receive your endowment, and kneel at the altar and are sealed, you can live an ordinary life and be an ordinary soul—struggling against temptation, failing and repenting, and failing again and repenting, but *always determined to keep your covenants*. . . . Then the day will come when you will receive the benediction: "Well done, thou good and faithful servant: thou hast been faithful over a few things, I will make thee ruler over many things: enter thou into the joy of thy Lord."[64]

In all of our learning, growing, struggling, and failing, it is necessary to keep both sides of the covenantal "coin" in mind. How we balance and integrate these concepts as we walk through life is something each of us must labor through individually, with help from the Lord. For me, a key to reconciling everything is found in Doctrine and Covenants 97:8, which reads, "Verily I say unto you, all . . . who know their hearts are honest, and are broken, and their spirits contrite, and are willing to observe their covenants by sacrifice—yea, every sacrifice which I, the Lord, shall command—they are accepted of me."

We need to repent. All of us can and should be seeking to improve and must rely on our Savior's grace as we stumble along. Overall, we generally have a sense of when our lives are on track and when we are off course. If you want to know your standing before the Lord, seek Him in prayer and ask Him to let you know. If you do so in faith, He will answer you.

Tokens

As part of the endowment, we also receive tokens and make a covenant in connection with them. Recognize that these tokens are symbols. And, like most temple symbols, they have multiple meanings. My wedding ring is a token of my marriage with my wife. Our actual marriage is something much greater than the ring. Be careful not to confuse the tokens of the temple with the greater realities they represent.

During the endowment presentation, these tokens are sent to us from God. They can mark certain points in our journey back to Him and provide a witness from God, accepting our covenants. As such, they represent stages in our development and relationship with God. The important thing is not simply receiving the symbol, but also recognizing and receiving what is *represented* by the symbol. God doesn't want us to only receive a ring when He intends for us to experience a joyous marriage.

The fact that the tokens are symbols doesn't diminish their sacredness. Some have broken their temple covenants by recording and posting the entire endowment ceremony on the Internet. (Having said that, please do not go to the Web to view the ceremony.) Anytime something is removed from its context and revealed, the original meaning is potentially lost or changed. Without the accompanying Spirit and an understanding of the symbolism, it may be easy to criticize the mechanics of gospel ordinances. The Lord intends for these ordinances to be given and received in a sacred, holy place built and consecrated for that purpose. He did not intend for anyone to receive his or her endowments via YouTube.

It is troubling that today anyone with enough curiosity may learn the endowment ceremony. However, once we recognize that the tokens given are just symbols, perhaps it doesn't matter if someone obtains them in an unauthorized manner. One can steal the symbol, but one cannot steal what is represented any more than someone stealing my wedding ring would also steal my marriage.

Still, the fact that others have broken their covenants and disclosed the entire ceremony does not remove from us who are endowed the obligation to maintain, in good faith, the confidence and sacredness of things we have covenanted not to disclose. We can still choose to be true and faithful to the obligations we've taken on ourselves, regardless of the choices of others. As LDS scholar Hugh Nibley explained, "The important thing is that I do not reveal these things; they must remain sacred to me . . . only I know exactly the weight and force of the covenants I have made—I and the Lord with whom I have made them . . . If I do not [reveal them], then they are secret and sacred no matter what others may say or do."[65]

Part of our being prepared to receive more is learning how to keep sacred that which we have already received. Joseph Smith taught, "The reason we do not have the secrets of the Lord revealed unto us, is because we do not keep them but reveal them."[66] I believe part of what we receive and are asked to keep confidential is a test, proving to God and ourselves that He can trust us. If we don't merit His confidence, nothing further will be given us.

Teachings

You also receive symbolic teaching and instruction as part of your endowment.[67] Elder James E. Talmage summarized,

> This course of instruction includes a recital of the most prominent events of the creative period, the condition of our first parents in the Garden of Eden, their disobedience and consequent expulsion from that blissful abode, their condition in the lone and dreary world when doomed to live by labor and sweat, the plan of redemption by which the great transgression may be atoned, the period of the great apostasy, the restoration of the gospel with all its ancient powers and privileges, the absolute and indispensable condition of personal purity and devotion to the right in present life, and a strict compliance with gospel requirements.[68]

Like an onion, the temple's teachings have layer upon layer of meaning. The endowment presents us with simple symbols, similar to what we find in Lehi's dream. And just as Nephi's subsequent vision revealed the depth and breadth of Lehi's dream, the temple symbols likewise contain much more than what initially appears on the surface. With that idea in mind, let's peel back a few of the layers.

Our discussion here will primarily be oriented around likening the temple's teachings to our own lives. However, doing so omits one of the fundamental purposes of the endowment. Just as the ordinances of the law of Moses were primarily intended to testify of Christ's sacrifice (see Alma 34:14), the temple endowment likewise can and does testify of Christ and His sacrifice in a more profound manner than we find anywhere else in the gospel. I would encourage you to seek to understand the temple's testimony of Christ, but the development of those ideas is well beyond our scope and purpose here. I point this out so that you can recognize one of the limitations of this book. The ideas that follow are simply given as a starting point in approaching the symbols of the endowment. There are additional meanings and interpretations beyond those discussed here.

The obvious approach is to view the endowment's teachings as history and simply see the story of Adam and Eve, the events of the Creation, the Fall, and so forth. Doing so provides insights into the origins of man and the conditions of mortality as established by God in the Garden of Eden. For many years, this was the only perspective from which I viewed the endowment. Then I began to recognize another layer of meaning.

You may also see in these teachings "your story." Or, in other words, as describing the condition into which you were born and find yourself in this life. Adam and Eve's story represents the journey each of us make through mortality. They are symbols. The story presented isn't the literal story of history but is symbolically teaching us about our own lives. Like our first parents, we were also created by God. We too began life in a state of innocence in our childhood. As we grew and matured, we were also tempted, tasted forbidden fruit, and fell. We lost our innocence and are learning by our own experiences the bitter and the sweet. We find ourselves cast out of God's presence, but we are given the choice to return. We must also offer the sacrifices the

Lord requires, call upon His name, receive true messengers, and learn to distinguish and reject false ones. We must also knock and converse with the Lord to return to His presence. With this perspective in mind, rather than trying to understand the temple in terms of X symbol represents Y thing, instead consider how X symbol relates to daily life and the world around us.

Taking this idea a little further, we may also view the events in the garden as an allegory. Adam and Eve can represent different parts of our individual nature. Regardless of whether you are male or female, each of us is in some ways like Adam and in other ways like Eve. We can consider ourselves as both Adam and Eve. Their actions, choices, and reactions may give us insights into our own behaviors.

For example, we may have a tendency to be rigid in our application of the commandments without checking with our loved ones and the Lord about our interpretation. Do we sometimes miss part of the picture, as Adam seemed to have done? Or do we rely upon our own wisdom or believe Satan's lies over God without checking again with Him for further knowledge, as Eve seemed to have done? We are each capable of both kinds of errors.

In marriage, do we ever risk disunity by ignoring our spouse and acting too independently, thereby failing to recognize that the image of God is both male and female together? Notice, too, the different spiritual strengths that each exhibits. How can we value the strengths of our spouse and grow together as one complete whole?

The story further highlights differences in the approach of the adversary. Each of us has a spiritual and physical side. Satan can some-times appeal to our physical nature when he cannot succeed with our spirits.[69] The temple endowment provides insight into our individual struggles in mortality.

Yet another window through which to view the temple is as an intersection point, where eternity and mortality meet. Upon enter-ing the temple, you are temporarily removed from the culture and context in which you live daily and are introduced into a different culture, one closer to that found on the other side of the veil. Pay attention to everything that surrounds you. What is the Lord trying to communicate? There is so much taught in the temple beyond just the audio and video presentation.

How might we bring some of the temple's culture into our daily lives and into our homes and families? The first great lesson of the endowment is presented as we are seated side by side, dressed in white. Think of the equality and fellowship represented in contrast with what we experience daily in the outside world, where we are constantly ranked, graded, and compared. While we can't control that, how easily and frequently does it also creep into our own thoughts and feelings? We are all guilty at times of comparing ourselves to others.

Pride and a poor self-image are two sides of the same coin. A proud man compares himself to others and feels superior, while a woman may compare herself to others and feel she doesn't measure up. The problem for both is in the false comparison. Nowhere in the scriptures are we commanded to compare ourselves to others. Rather, the scriptures admonish us to think of our brethren like unto ourselves (see Jacob 2:17). This simple, basic truth is powerfully presented to us in the temple. Do we have eyes to really see? Imagine how our world and society would change if this one truth were widely lived. While that may not be possible, how might we go about it in our own individual lives and interactions with others? If Zion consists of those who are of one heart and mind, the temple can help prepare us for that environment.

Lastly, recognize the temple endowment as your own personal Liahona. Consider anew a well-known scripture: "Know ye not that *ye are the temple of God*, and that the Spirit of God dwelleth in you?" (1 Corinthians 3:16; emphasis added). You've likely heard this scripture repeated often. Pause and think about it carefully. What if Paul wasn't just employing an analogy? Perhaps he meant exactly what he said. *You are the temple of God.* What if your *real* endowment is your life? Your life and the opportunity to become a holy temple are the true gifts you have been endowed with by God.

When seen from that perspective, everything changes. Your temple endowment then provides a map or blueprint for your journey through life. It outlines the path Adam and Eve and others followed to receive their exaltation. It extends to you the same blessings, promises, and invitations from the Lord. The endowment teaches you of things He wants you to receive and endows you with the power to receive them. When you understand what is being symbolized, the endowment, like the Liahona, can point the way and give you new instructions and insights from time to time as you find your way back into His presence.

When the Church builds a new temple, a detailed blueprint is first drawn up. The actual physical construction then proceeds, according to the plan. The Salt Lake Temple took forty years to complete. Likewise, the creation of the earth was first spiritual and then physical (see Moses 3:5). What you receive in your temple endowment is like a blueprint. It is a spiritual creation, which should precede an actual physical creation in your life. You are to become a holy temple.

The events you enact ceremonially in the endowment are intended for you to experience in reality as well. Don't mistake the blueprint for the actual construction. The ordinance and the symbols are important, but they are not the final things. Try to see and understand the underlying realities that are portrayed in the temple endowment. More importantly, seek for their fulfillment in your life.

Milestones in Your Journey

With the idea in mind that your day-to-day life is your real endowment and that the temple endowment provides you with a blueprint or map for your journey, let's look at four gifts you may potentially receive along the way. These four gifts are the light of Christ, baptism of fire and the Holy Ghost, your calling and election made sure, and the Second Comforter. Though these are gifts sent from God, we might also view them as milestones and helps along our path.

In the endowment ceremony, we receive four tokens. Jeremy Oakes in his book *The Journey* linked the symbolism of the four tokens with these four gifts.[70] He further suggested that once we view the tokens as representing these gifts or milestones, we can ask the Lord to show us where we are in our own journey. If you will attend an endowment session and ask the Lord in faith to let you know where you are at in your progression, He will let you know. That understanding can help us glimpse what still lies ahead or what we lack, along with the recognition of what we have already received. In this manner, the endowment can provide us with our bearings in our daily wilderness, much as the Liahona did for Lehi's family.

I like and agree with Jeremy's thoughts, and we will further explore this interpretation in the remainder of this chapter. However, I would also reiterate once again that these four gifts are not the only things symbolized by the tokens. The tokens have other meanings as well. Use this interpretation if it seems helpful to you and discard it if it does not.

Gift 1: The Light of Christ

The first gift or token is one we all receive. The scriptures testify that the light of Christ proceeds "forth from the presence of God to fill the immensity of space" and is the "light which is in all things, which giveth life to all things" and "the law by which all things are governed" (D&C 88:12–13). The light of Christ gives life to everything. All of creation is connected to the Creator. King Benjamin testified that God "created you from the beginning, and is preserving you from day to day, by lending you breath, that ye may live and move and do according to your own will, and even supporting you from one moment to another" (Mosiah 2:21).

Each of us is intimately connected to God. He is giving us life day by day. As you sit here reading this book, you are at this moment connected with God, whether you are aware of it or not. This connection is one reason He communicates with us through our thoughts and feelings. Our sense of isolation and privacy is an illusion. God respects our agency and largely remains quiet until—and unless—we invite Him into our lives. He is willing to be talkative if we will permit and listen. We will talk about some ways to do this in chapter six.

One way that the light of Christ manifests itself is by acting as our conscience. We receive this gift as we begin to grow and become accountable. Adam and Eve received this token before being driven out of God's immediate presence in the Garden of Eden. Though they had fallen and would no longer be in His immediate presence, they would retain this connection to Him. It is the same for us. Though it may seem a small thing at times, listening to this guide will help us grow in light and truth. Or we can choose to ignore and dull it. Either way, everyone who is accountable receives it. "For behold, the Spirit of Christ is given to every man, that he may know good from evil" (Moroni 7:16).

Gift 2: Baptism of Fire and the Holy Ghost

Unlike the first gift, which is nearly universal, the second—receiving the baptism of fire and the Holy Ghost—is conditional. Nephi taught, "For the gate by which ye should enter is repentance and baptism by water; and then cometh a remission of your sins by fire and by the Holy Ghost. And then are ye in this strait and narrow path which leads to eternal life" (2 Nephi 31:17–18).

After we are baptized, the ordinance of confirmation places upon us an obligation to receive the Holy Ghost. It is interesting that the scriptures refer to this as a baptism of fire *and* the Holy Ghost (see 3 Nephi 9:20). Why are both mentioned? Why is it a baptism of fire, not just a baptism of the Holy Ghost? In the scriptures, fire is associated with acceptance of a sacrifice. It purges and cleanses. And fire is often present with the opening of the heavens. For example, both Lehi and Joseph Smith encountered a pillar of fire in their experiences.

As members of the LDS faith, we tend to most often speak of the Holy Ghost as a comforter, and that is one of its functions. It is the first Comforter. You have probably felt from time to time that peace that only comes from God through this Comforter. As an example,

Oliver Cowdery was reminded of the night God spoke peace unto Oliver's soul concerning the work (see D&C 6:22–23). This peace may be hard to explain to someone, but it is unmistakable when felt.

The Holy Ghost's role and influence are not exclusively manifested through our feelings. It is also a revelator. Joseph Smith taught that the Holy Ghost's effect is intelligence and that it expands our minds and enlightens our understanding.[71] The Holy Ghost communicates with us. We receive direction, guidance, understanding, and revelation in our lives through its influence. This is something greater than a *feeling* we experience. Some have criticized members' testimonies as being based upon something they perceive to be as flimsy as a *feeling* while not understanding that the Holy Ghost's role is also to enlighten and reveal.

In addition, the Holy Ghost is a sanctifier. We are sanctified (made holy) by its reception and influence (see 3 Nephi 27:20). This is one reason it is so important to seek this influence in our lives. The scriptures invite us to grow up in the Lord and receive a fulness of the Holy Ghost (see D&C 109:15). Helping us to do so is one part of the temple's purpose.

Most members of the Church have felt or experienced the Holy Ghost's influence. But is that the same thing as receiving the baptism of fire and the Holy Ghost? And is that baptism a distinct event, like the baptism by water, or is it a process that is gradual and occurs over time?

When Christ visited the Nephites, He taught, "And ye shall offer for a sacrifice unto me a broken heart and a contrite spirit. [Notice this is the condition to receiving this baptism.] And whoso cometh unto me with a broken heart and a contrite spirit, him will I baptize with fire and with the Holy Ghost, even as the Lamanites, because of their faith in me at the time of their conversion, were baptized with fire and with the Holy Ghost, and *they knew it not*" (3 Nephi 9:20; emphasis added). Now that is odd; how could the Lamanites receive this baptism and not know it? Was the experience so subtle they didn't realize anything had happened? Or was it something they definitely experienced but didn't recognize for what it was?

These seem to be important questions. You can study these things out and reach your own conclusions. In my opinion, the full baptism of fire and the Holy Ghost is both an event and a process, though I would use a different term for the process. I would refer to the process as becoming sanctified, the mighty change of heart, being reborn, or receiving a fulness of the Holy Ghost. But I also believe that the baptism of fire and the Holy Ghost is a single event, distinct as the baptism of water. Though it can, I don't believe it necessarily happens automatically at the time we were confirmed members of the Church by the laying on of hands. At that time, we were admonished to *receive the Holy Ghost.*

I was raised in the Church by good parents, was baptized by water at eight, and have remained active throughout my life. I was endowed in the temple at nineteen and served an honorable mission. Throughout those years, I experienced manifestations of the Holy Ghost. On the day I was endowed, I left the temple having felt the Holy Ghost to a greater degree than ever before. But it was not until I was thirty that I received the baptism of fire and the Holy Ghost.

On October 14, 1996, I was in the temple and experienced a taste of the joy that awaits us hereafter. I was filled as with fire from the crown of my head to the soles of my feet. I received a remission of my sins at that time. It was the most sacred and significant experience of my life to that point in time. Though, like the Lamanites, I did not recognize it for what it was until many years later. Others have had similar experiences.

Perhaps this baptism manifests itself in various ways for different people, because we are all unique individuals. Maybe for some it is not recognizable as a distinct event. However, my guess is that for many baptized members of the Church, this remains a yet future event in their lives. It is something God would have all of us receive. It is a critical part of our journey back. Adam also needed this baptism to return to the Lord's presence and received this token some time after being cast out of the garden (see Moses 6:66).

Read Nephi's testimony carefully: "For the gate by which ye should enter is repentance and baptism by water; and then cometh a remission of your sins by fire and by the Holy Ghost. *And then are ye in this strait and narrow path* which leads to eternal life" (2 Nephi 31:17–18; emphasis added). We think of baptism as putting us on the path, but Nephi plainly indicated that we are not even on the straight and narrow path until *after* we have been baptized by fire and the Holy Ghost. This is a critical matter to our salvation. If you are uncertain, ask God to reveal to you whether you have received this baptism. The Lord has promised that if we come to him with a broken heart and a contrite spirit, we will receive it (see 3 Nephi 9:20).

Gift 3: Your Calling and Election Made Sure

After we have been baptized by fire and the Holy Ghost, we are to be led by the Spirit in our lives. We are promised that it will show us all things we are to do (see 2 Nephi 32:5). As we press forward through life, seeking and relying upon the guidance of the Holy Ghost, the next big milestone in our journey home is to have our calling and election made sure. This topic is perhaps widely misunderstood among members of the Church. Though the Prophet Joseph Smith openly taught the subject, it is not emphasized today.[72] The purpose here is not to fully delve into it, but rather simply to introduce the concept and plant a seed in your heart.

For some members of the Church, the topics of calling and election and the Second Comforter raise some anxiety. Some caution and restraint is certainly prudent. There are two sides of the "coin" here, just as we encountered with covenants. First, we will consider some of the doctrine. I would humbly ask that if this topic causes you concern or fear, please set that aside momentarily and see if the following discussion can be helpful. After we have looked at the teaching and doctrine on these subjects, we will return to address some concerns and potential pitfalls. We should try to understand both sides of the coin.

Peter admonished those in his day to "give diligence to make your calling and election sure: for if ye do these things, ye shall never fall: for so an entrance shall be ministered unto you abundantly into the everlasting kingdom of our Lord and Saviour Jesus Christ" (2 Peter 1:10–11).

This is Peter, the Lord's chief Apostle. He was urging the Saints to diligently seek to make their calling and election sure so that they would not fall. He continued his epistle by stating that he was going to continually remind them of these things: "Wherefore I will not be negligent to put you always in remembrance of these things, though ye know them. . . . Yea, I think it meet, as long as I am in this taber-nacle, to stir you up by putting you in remembrance" (2 Peter 1:12–13). Receiving their calling and election was so critically important that Peter planned to remind them and stir them up as long as he lived. And yet today, we scarcely hear mention of the matter.

So what exactly is it? Think back to the initiatory ordinances of the temple. What is the *calling and election* you received there? What would it mean to have that calling *made sure*? The scriptures teach, "The more sure word of prophecy [calling and election] means a man's knowing that he is sealed up unto eternal life, by revelation and the spirit of prophecy, through the power of the Holy Priesthood" (D&C 131:5).

Does this mean we have to be perfect to receive it? Absolutely not. Otherwise no one would ever receive this blessing in his or her lifetime. Remember Nephi's lamentation: "O wretched man that I am! Yea, my heart sorroweth because of my flesh; my soul grieveth because of mine iniquities. I am encompassed about, because of the temptations and the sins which do so easily beset me" (2 Nephi 4:17–18). Nephi still struggled in a way we can all relate to, and this was after his incredible spiritual experiences.

This gift and our salvation are not things we earn. They are gifts of grace. Perfection is not required. We need to qualify, but that is different from earning. The scriptures make it clear that because of the Fall, we can't "earn" anything on our own merits, no matter how "good" we are (see Alma 22:14). We live in a fallen world, sur-rounded by sin. It's like being in the bottom of a deep, dark pit. We aren't going to climb out on our own. We are never going to save ourselves. We all need the Savior to rescue us! Our hearts become broken and our spirits contrite as we recognize our total and com-plete inadequacy and humble ourselves before God. We need Him to change our natures and desires, but even then we will still fall short in mortality. Like Nephi, we must come to know in whom we trust (see 2 Nephi 4:19).

So how do we qualify to receive this hope? How do we receive the promise of eternal life? Joseph Smith received this more sure word of prophecy from God. The Lord told him, "I am the Lord thy God, and will be with thee even unto the end of the world, and through all eternity; for verily I seal upon you your exaltation, and prepare a throne for you in the kingdom of my Father, with Abraham your father" (D&C 132:49). Here, we see an example in the scriptures of the Lord Himself making this promise directly. Imagine the hope and comfort this testimony gave to Joseph.

Still, we may wonder if it is really possible for a normal member of the Church to receive such a promise from the Lord. You might be thinking to yourself something like, *Okay. But that was Joseph Smith. And he was a prophet. And I'm just not like him. Joseph was way up there, and I'm way down here. I'll never be like him.* Fair enough. But consider another example from the Book of Mormon. The Lord also said to Alma, "Thou art my servant; and I covenant with thee that thou shalt have eternal life" (Mosiah 26:20). This was Alma, the wicked priest of King Noah. The same Alma who was so far off course in his earlier life. Yet, here he received a covenant and promise of eternal life directly from the Lord.

This blessing didn't come to Alma because he held a high leadership position. It didn't come to him because he lived a life free of mistakes and regrets. And he wasn't perfect at the time he received this promise. It came because he had faith in the word of the Lord, delivered by Abinadi. That testimony led Alma to repent and serve the Lord. Alma began seeking to do the Lord's will. Eventually, he received this promise and blessing directly from the Lord—and it came quietly as Alma went about his service.

How is this possible? We might well ask, like Enos, "Lord, how is it done?" (Enos 1:7). We can feel so weak and flawed and hopelessly human. Why would Peter give us a commandment to seek after something that may seem so far out of our reach? How can we ever obtain it? The answer is the same as the one given to Enos: "*Because of thy faith* in Christ, whom thou hast never before heard nor seen" (Enos 1:8; emphasis added). We aren't perfect. But we can develop our faith to the point that it is sufficient and acceptable to the Lord.

Paul testified, "For by *grace* are ye saved *through faith*; and that not of yourselves: it is the gift of God" (Ephesians 2:8; emphasis added). We came here to develop faith. Ultimately, it is your faith that you contribute toward your salvation. Paul's statement is correct. However, many have not understood the kind of faith referred to.

Joseph Smith did. He understood this is not the initial seed of faith but the mature tree of faith (see Alma 32). Lest we think this easy, he taught in the *Lectures on Faith*: "Let us here observe that *a religion that does not require the sacrifice of all things never has power sufficient to produce the faith necessary* unto life and salvation."[73] The Prophet Joseph continued, "It is through this sacrifice, *and this only,* that God has ordained that men should enjoy eternal life."[74] We can only be saved once we possess this kind of faith. We can only receive this faith through sacrifice. Faith grows through obedience and sacrifice. That may explain the purpose behind some of the temple covenants we have made.

Sacrifice of this type is rarely given in one fell swoop. Rather, it is given over our lifetime. We sacrifice day by day as we strive to live the gospel and raise families in righteousness. It often requires sacrifice for us to do the Lord's will. Missionaries sacrifice early in their lives as they leave their homes and all they know to serve the Lord. This may seem a wintry doctrine—and in some ways it is. But sacrifice is not something we should fear. It generally brings forth greater blessings than what was offered up. Most missionaries can testify that what they gained by serving a mission far exceeds anything they had given up in sacrifice of it.

Still, we might question with Eve if there is not some easier path, to which the answer remains the same. There is no other way. It is not easy, but it is possible. Others have done so, and you can too. Saving faith is mature faith. It is a faith you have nurtured from a seed to a mighty tree, which then produces fruit. Small incremental sacrifices are required all along the gospel path. They are necessary to help faith grow and develop.

If you seek these blessings, then at some point in your progression, the Lord will require a sacrifice of you, one which is personal and likely uniquely customized for you. This sacrifice is not something you can invent or offer on your own. It will be something the Lord requires you to lay upon the altar as you seek to do His will in your life. It will be both a test and a blessing to you. The Lord knows when you are ready and will supply the test Himself through the individual circumstances of your life. You may not even recognize it for what it is until after it is over.

Once you have made this sacrifice, you will know that you are accepted of the Lord. Joseph Smith testified, "When a man [or woman] has offered in sacrifice all that he [or she] has for the truth's sake, not even withholding his life, and believing before God that he has been called to make this sacrifice because he seeks to do his will, he does know, most assuredly, that God does and will accept his sacrifice and offering, and that he has not, nor will not seek his face in vain."[75]

You might feel all of this is simply out of your reach, that it's just not possible. Maybe a few of the early Saints in Joseph's day received these things, but it doesn't happen today. And yet, remember Peter gave a commandment in the scriptures to seek these things diligently. It is a commandment to all of us—a commandment from one who knew what he was talking about and who is inviting and pleading with us to do the same. And as Nephi would emphatically remind us, we are never given a commandment without a way to accomplish it (see 1 Nephi 3:7). God will help you if you will move forward in faith. Plant a seed in your heart and allow it to grow.

If it were not within our reach, why would Peter have been preaching these things? Why would he think it important enough not only to preach them but also to continually remind those in his day of these things? And if we think it applied to them and doesn't apply to us, Joseph Smith made it more so. He stated, "You have got to make your calling and election sure. If this injunction would lie largely on those to whom it was spoken, how much more [to] those of the present generation!"[76]

These blessings are available today and can be received by normal, everyday members of the Church. God is no respecter of persons. He desires all to receive these things. Come to Him in your weakness and let Him heal you. Press forward in faith until your calling and election are made sure by Him. Peter knew what he was teaching.

You don't have to hold a high Church leadership position to qualify. Those who receive their calling and election directly from the Lord are among the ordinary members of the Church. Peter and Joseph both imply that this blessing should not be something exceptional, but rather it should be a more common experience among members of the Church. The endowment also testifies it is possible. It is within the reach of most who will read this book. In the final two chapters, we will discuss practical suggestions that can assist you to also receive this blessing.

I close with this admonition from the Prophet Joseph Smith: "I would exhort you to go on and continue to call upon God until you make your calling and election sure for yourselves, by obtaining this more sure word of prophecy, and wait patiently for the promise until you obtain it."[77]

Gift 4: The Second Comforter

"And ye shall seek me, and find me, when ye shall search for me with all your heart" (Jeremiah 29:13). The gospel and the doctrine of Christ are intended to bring us back into His presence. Joseph Smith summarized the entire process as follows:

> After a person has faith in Christ, repents of his sins, and is baptized for the remission of his sins and receives the Holy Ghost, (by the laying on of hands), which is the first Comforter, then let him continue to humble himself before God, hungering and thirsting after righteousness, and living by every word of God, and the Lord will soon say unto him, Son [or daughter], thou shalt be exalted.
>
> When the Lord has thoroughly proved him, and finds that the man [or woman] is determined to serve Him at all hazards, then the man will find his calling and his election made sure, then it will be his privilege to receive the other Comforter, which the Lord hath promised the Saints. . . .
>
> Now what is this other Comforter? It is no more nor less than the Lord Jesus Christ Himself; and this is the sum and substance of the whole matter; that when any man obtains this last Comforter, he will have the personage of Jesus Christ to attend him, or appear unto him from time to time, and even He will manifest the Father unto him, and they will take up their abode with him, and the visions of the heavens will be opened unto him, and the Lord will teach him face to face, and he may have a perfect knowledge of the mysteries of the Kingdom of God.[78]

With the idea in mind that we are to become a holy temple of God, remember that the Lord visits His temples. The scriptures promise that "the Lord, whom ye seek, shall suddenly come to his temple" (Malachi 3:1).

We tend to think of these things in terms of the next life. However, Elder Bruce R. McConkie testified, "The purpose of the endowment in the house of the Lord is to prepare and sanctify his saints so they will be able to see his face, *here and now*, as well as to bear the glory of his presence in the eternal worlds."[79]

Perhaps the one verse in all of scripture that summarizes the temple endowment best is Doctrine and Covenants 93:1: "Verily, thus saith the Lord: It shall come to pass that *every soul* who forsaketh his sins and cometh unto me, and calleth on my name, and obeyeth my voice, and keepeth my commandments, shall see my face and know that I am" (emphasis added). "Every soul" includes you. The return to Christ's presence is what you ceremonially enact in the endowment. You should receive Christ in this mortal life (see 2 Nephi 32:6, D&C 132:22–23). There is no mention of dying before you are presented at the veil in the endowment ceremony.

About this point, you might be thinking something like, *I've never heard of anyone having this experience before. Is it really true?* Turn to the scriptures and you will see example after example. Right in the opening of the Book of Mormon, we find it in Lehi's experience. Nephi, in his writings, testified of the same and outlined the path he followed to receive these blessings.

Centuries before Lehi, Moses also stood in the presence of God. Following his experience, Moses wanted to sanctify all of the children of Israel so they could receive the same blessing. With a few exceptions, he failed in this attempt. The ancient Israelites rejected what was offered them and angered the Lord (see D&C 84:23–24). Eventually, Moses was taken out of their midst, but he left behind commandments and ordinances.

After Moses, generation after generation of Israelites lived and died. They participated in the ordinances left by Moses but—for the most part—failed to understand their intent and purpose. They did not see the testimony and invitation contained in the ordinances. But in Lehi, we encounter an Israelite who succeeded in receiving what Moses intended for all the children of Israel. Lehi was redeemed and returned to the Lord's presence. Why did he succeed when so many others did not? What made Lehi different?

Not only Lehi, but Nephi, Jacob, and Enos also received these things. And so on right down through the Book of Mormon until we come to the brother of Jared and Mormon and Moroni.[80] From beginning to end, the Book of Mormon testifies over and over of these things.

In our day, Joseph Smith sought to bring the same blessings to modern Israel in Nauvoo. He didn't fare much better in the attempt than Moses. Eventually, Joseph was also taken. He also left behind ordinances. What is the purpose of the temple ordinances Joseph restored? Generations of Saints have participated in the ordinances left by Joseph, and many failed to understand their intent and purpose. Recognize in them an invitation for you to rise up and return to the Lord's presence.

There are those in our day who have received these blessings as well. However, not everyone who has seen the Lord also received his or her calling and election. These are two different things. Speaking of Peter, James, and John on the Mount of Transfiguration, Joseph Smith taught, "It is one thing to be on the mount and hear the excellent voice, etc., and another to hear the voice declare to you, you have a part and lot in that kingdom."[81]

Christ's visit to you is not to satisfy your curiosity. He has a ministry to perform, which He reserves to Himself. Jacob testified, "The keeper of the gate is the Holy One of Israel; and he employeth no servant there; and there is none other way save it be by the gate" (2 Nephi 9:41).

As part of the doctrine of Christ, Nephi admonished, "Feast upon the words of Christ; for behold, the words of Christ will tell you all things what ye should do . . . again I say unto you that if ye will enter in by the way, and receive the Holy Ghost, it will show unto you all things what ye should do. Behold, this is the doctrine of Christ, and there will be no more doctrine given *until after he shall manifest himself unto you in the flesh. And when he shall manifest himself unto you in the flesh, the things which he shall say unto you shall ye observe to do*" (2 Nephi 32:3, 5–6; emphasis added).[82]

Now, a few words of caution. Before we conclude our discussion of calling and election and the Second Comforter, let's look at the other side of the coin. One reason members may have concern with these topics is because of those who have "gone off the deep end." People do and believe some wacky things.

These blessings are given to and received by the humble followers of Christ. They come about in the Lord's time and by His will as these disciples go about humbly seeking to serve, as did Alma, and are given for their personal blessing (see D&C 88:68).

If you receive them, they will probably come about as a quiet reassurance from the Lord. They provide a hope that the scriptures often refer to as entering into the rest of the Lord. They are to bless your life. They will not give you the right to set yourself up as a spiritual authority, or as a light for others to follow. Nor do they give you the right to direct your ward or stake or anything else. That is not their purpose. Rather, they are intended to give you a firm hope in your journey home.

Many, perhaps even most, who have received these blessings never speak of or testify of them simply because they are so sacred and personal. Others are given permission or even an admonition to share them. Lehi testified openly of his experiences to the unbelieving Jews of his day, as did many of the prophets.

Recognize though that, like the ancient prophets in the Book of Mormon, anyone who truly has received these blessings is going to invite others to repent and point them to Christ. They will not be seeking to build themselves up but will be seeking to testify, teach, and lift up and serve others. They recognize their weaknesses before God and do not feel themselves more elect than others. In fact, it is my opinion that if anyone claims to have received these blessings and uses them as "credentials" to build themselves up as a light and encourage others to follow them, it should be a bright red flag for the rest of us. We are to follow the Savior.

Lehi's experience was authentic. Following it, his message was repentance and to testify of the Messiah. His testimony was rejected and caused him personal suffering. Nephi experienced the same. Their ministry was the opposite of priestcraft, which seeks popularity, recognition, acclaim, and honor.

Because of these things, when approaching these topics, a level of caution is wise. However, we should not allow a prudent caution to turn into fear that prevents us from first understanding, then seeking, and eventually receiving blessings the Lord wants for us to receive.

The Veil of the Temple

The endowment ceremony concludes with symbolically conversing with the Lord and being admitted into His presence. It is the most sacred part of the ceremony. Before finishing our discussion of the endowment, let us briefly consider the temple veil.

The purpose of a veil is to cover that which is most sacred. In other words, what is behind the veil is too sacred to be revealed to everyone. The veil in Moses's tabernacle and Solomon's temple shielded the Holy of Holies from view. Only the high priest was permitted to enter in and then only under specific conditions and purposes (see Leviticus 16). Likewise, we find places in the scriptures where a veil is drawn over what a prophet can share in his record and the additional knowledge he would like to give is withheld (see, for example, 2 Nephi 32:7; 3 Nephi 26:11; 28:25).

When Moses descended from speaking with the Lord on Mount Sinai, he was so filled with the glory of God that his face shone, and the children of Israel were afraid to come near him (see Exodus 34:29–30). Moses placed a veil over his face to cover this glory until he finished speaking with them (see Exodus 34:33).

In our day, a bride is traditionally veiled prior to her marriage, and in some parts of the world, it is customary for women to be veiled as part of their daily attire. In Western cultures, some view the veiling of women in a negative light, seeing it as placing women in an inferior position to men. These negative connotations sometimes give rise to questions about our endowment ceremony, which includes a veil as part of the ceremonial clothing worn by the women. Perhaps this negative association stems largely from a lack of understanding of the significance of veils. Anciently—along with virtue, chastity, and obedience to God—veils also symbolized divinely recognized power or authority.[83]

One of the reasons women are veiled at a certain point in the endowment ceremony is to remind us of their divine nature and glory. I believe some things about women and their role in eternity are simply too sacred to yet be revealed to the world, or even to the Saints, and so remain veiled. Like the scriptural records of the prophets, we reach a point in the endowment where greater things are implied but withheld, and a veil is drawn until we are prepared to receive more (see 3 Nephi 26:9–10). The veiling of women in the endowment is not to diminish them in the least; it is precisely the opposite. We are reminded of their divine value. Like Moses, their glory is presently covered.

The veil of the temple also protects that which is most sacred. In the ceremony, we are permitted to enter within the veil, following some testing and preparation. The temple veil is richly symbolic with a variety of meanings. Consider a few of them. As mentioned earlier, one thing the veil symbolizes is Christ (see Hebrews 10:19–20). This is appropriate because we can only return to the Father through Christ. As a symbol of Christ, the veil also denotes the tree of life. Earlier in the presentation, we encountered the tree of knowledge and, symbolically through Adam and Eve, partook of its fruit. At the endowment's conclusion, in the temple veil, we find embodied the tree of life and are presented there to receive its fruit.

The veil of Moses's tabernacle was colorful, woven with blue, purple, scarlet, and linen threads (see Exodus 36:35). These four colors all pointed to Christ.[84] Blue suggested the celestial realms and Christ's condescension in coming to earth. Purple was the color of royalty and majesty, and it marked someone of high rank or authority. Scarlet reminded Israel of Christ's blood shed in sacrifice. Linen reflected His purity and holiness.

In addition to these symbols of Christ, the four colors also represent the four elements from the Creation of the world: earth (linen), air (blue), water (purple), and fire (scarlet).[85] (Or, alternatively, the states of matter—solid, liquid, gaseous, and energy.)

As such, the veil represents the Creation. The veil forms a boundary between heaven and earth. Or, we might say, it is a division between the physical and spiritual realms. And it also indicates a division between time and eternity.

But the symbolism is not limited to the Creation of this earth alone. When Enoch spoke with God, he marveled at all of His creations. Enoch exclaimed, "And were it possible that man could number the particles of the earth, yea, millions of earths like this, it would not be a beginning to the number of thy creations; and *thy curtains* are stretched out still" (see Moses 7:30; emphasis added). The curtain (or veil) denoted all of God's Creation. The entire physical universe, and all of God's continuing works, are also suggested by the temple veil.

These are some of the positive symbols associated with the veil, but there are negative ones as well. The temple veil also stands for things that bar us from the Lord's presence. It represents our unbelief, and we must all "rend" this veil (see Ether 4:15). Unbelief refers not just to lack of belief, but also to things we believe that aren't true. We are all afflicted to some degree with unbelief as a result of the things we learn and experience while growing up in this fallen world.

On top of this, our individual *veil of unbelief* is reinforced by our fears, pride, jealousies, hard hearts, and sins (see D&C 67:10; Alma 5:28). We must work to set all these things aside and reach up to God, even as He reaches down to each of us. Doing so can seem almost beyond our reach. It can be so hard to give Him our doubts and fears and put our complete trust in the Lord. And yet, the temple testifies that as we knock, the Lord will reach through the veil of our unbelief and fear and take us by the hand while we journey through life. If we will then prove faithful to the things He requires of us, in His own time, the Lord can and will part this veil and bring us back into His presence (see D&C 88:68).

Part of the required rending is to plant the seed in your heart so that it is possible to return to the Lord's presence and be redeemed while still mortal. The scriptures testify to us over and over again that it is possible for each of us. God is no respecter of persons, and yet we are so slow to believe Him.

These blessings are available if we seek them. Joseph Smith testified it is possible. And the temple endowment not only testifies it can be done, but it also shows us the way. Whether we receive these blessings is largely up to us. We must awake and arise to our awful situation. We must forsake unbelief and seek truth. We must repent, turn our hearts and minds to God, become clean, and exercise faith (see Ether 4:6–7).

The temple endowment ceremony concludes as we pass through the veil and enter the celestial room. Here, we symbolically stand back in the presence of the Lord. We have passed through various stages and levels of ascent to arrive in this holy place. As we enter the celestial room, may our reverence reflect the sacredness of the place. May we also be sensitive to those who are there seeking peace and solace from the storms of life or who may be there seeking a quiet place apart to commune with their Lord.

Homework

1. Resolve today to press forward, seeking to come unto Christ until your calling and election is made sure by Him. We will discuss some practical steps to help you in the final chapter of this book, but make the resolution today.

2. Attend an endowment session. Ask the Lord to show you where you are in your development. What is the next step for you? Listen for His Spirit to prompt you. He will let you know. Used in this way, the temple can give you your bearings in what you have received and what you may still lack. Jeremy Oakes testified, "As I went to the temple I would often ask, 'Where am I in the journey?' At some point in the ceremony He would answer, 'Here.' I would evaluate what was happening in my life at that time. Slowly the endowment and initiatory ceremony began to take the shape of a personal journey."[86] I have taken Jeremy's suggestion and testify that it works.

3. Have you been baptized by fire and the Holy Ghost? If not, how could you come unto Him with a broken heart and a contrite spirit in order to receive it?

4. Learn the covenants you make as part of the endowment. How can you live them more fully in your life? Regardless of what others may be doing, how can you consecrate yourself more fully to the Lord?

5. Study the *Lectures on Faith*. These lectures outline the doctrine of faith and contain crucial teachings in relation to these topics.

6. We have only glimpses of Lehi's life and do not see what he went through before his vision. However, we do have more detail in the account of the brother of Jared. Study it carefully. You

will find all of the major elements of the temple endowment portrayed in his life's story.[87] The endowment story is the story of your Fall and your potential redemption from the Fall. Finding redemption is being brought back into the Lord's presence (Ether 3:13). The brother of Jared received these blessings because of his "exceeding faith" (Ether 3:9). You are promised that you can receive the same (Ether 4:7).

7. Study "The Light of Christ" by Marion G. Romney (*Ensign*, April 1977).

CHAPTER 5

Temple Sealings

"Neither is the man without the woman, neither the woman without the man, in the Lord."

—1 Corinthians 11:11

I s there a difference between a temple wedding and a temple marriage? After creating Adam, God declared that it was not good for man to be alone (Genesis 2:18). This remains true today. No matter what he might accomplish or what other qualities he may possess, man cannot be wholly acceptable in God's sight while single and alone.

Eve remedied Adam's condition. Together, they could have children and further God's purposes. When joined by God, they became whole and potentially infinite. The image of God is both male and female (Genesis 1:27). The Garden of Eden served as the world's first temple. It was in this setting that God joined Adam and Eve in the holy covenant of marriage. He intended this covenant to be eternal. It was formed before the Fall and death entered the world.

Furthermore, Adam knew that Eve was to *remain* with him (Moses 4:18). Through all of life's ups and downs, through happy times and sad ones, and through all of the challenges and opposition that arise in even the best of marriages, God intended for marriage partners to remain together. Christ reiterated this during His mortal ministry. He stated, "For this cause shall a man leave father and mother, and shall cleave to his wife. . . . Wherefore they are no more twain, but one flesh. What therefore God hath joined together, let not man put asunder" (Matthew 19:5–6).

Joseph Smith gave further insights into God's ultimate purpose for marriage. "In the celestial glory there are three heavens or degrees; and in order to obtain the highest, a man must enter into this order of the priesthood [meaning the new and everlasting covenant of marriage]; and if he does not, he cannot obtain it. He may enter into the other, but that is the end of his kingdom; he cannot have an increase" (D&C 131:1–4). As repentance and baptism are the gate leading to eternal life (2 Nephi 31:17–18), so eternal marriage is the gate leading to exaltation.

All of the prior gospel ordinances build up to and prepare us for our temple sealing. Our temple wedding is a similitude of Adam and Eve's. When we enter the celestial room of a temple, we symbolically stand in the presence of God. The temple's sealing rooms are extensions of and therefore part of the celestial room.[88] The ordinance is performed in the symbolic presence of God. A new and potentially everlasting covenant is formed.

On your wedding day, you receive the same potential blessings of exaltation as were given to Adam and Eve, Abram and Sarai, and others, but now they are given from God to you and your spouse. You leave the temple having obtained the same promises, but they are given conditionally. While the power behind a temple sealing is real, receiving the promised blessings will depend upon your subsequent faithfulness. So what exactly do you leave the temple with on your wedding day?

As a child, I remember my mother spending hours in the kitchen, canning fruits and vegetables from our garden into glass Mason jars to preserve them. We always loved getting a jar of her peaches out of the pantry and enjoying them on a cold winter evening. Michael Wilcox compared being sealed in the temple to receiving an empty glass jar.[89] The sealing ordinances provide you with the promises and potential, or the empty jar. But it is up to each couple to fill their jar during their lifetime together. With any luck, things such as love, children, laughter, work, service, joy, tears and sorrow, struggle and triumph, and wonderful memories will go into our jars, so that before the end of our lives, we possess something that is worth the Lord sealing up for all eternity.

How can we do that? There are so many failures. Some challenges are built into marriage because it begins with two people from different backgrounds and families. Each brings his and her unique strengths and weaknesses and ideas of how things should be. Add to all of this the inherent differences between the sexes, and the work of raising a family and marriage can be a real challenge. How can the two ever hope to become one?

It's tough at times. We all grow up hearing fairy tales, where the prince slays the dragon, rescues the princess, and they live happily ever after. Young couples often overcome obstacles and adversity before beginning their lives together, only to discover that the real struggle is still to come. Opposition in all things. There is a joy waiting on the other side of overcoming adversity that comes in no other way. Marriage is given for the growth and development of both spouses. Sometimes, the problems we encounter in marriage are the circumstances we need to grapple with for our growth and development. Sometimes, one partner throws in the towel, thinking the grass looks greener in other pastures, only to find themselves in another relationship or marriage, once again facing similar issues.

The covenants made in the endowment provide the foundation to build a successful marriage. The only way to find true happiness in a marriage is for both spouses to commit to putting God first in their lives and their relationship with each other right after, and then going to work on that each day. It is in sacrifice and serving your partner that your individual happiness and growth emerges almost as a byproduct. The best place to practice living the principles of the gospel is in our own marriages and families. Your spouse is not given to satisfy you but for you to learn to love.

Oneness in marriage comes from respecting, fostering, and encouraging each other's individuality and growth and coming together into oneness of heart with the Lord's purposes. A covenant marriage is spiritually based. Your temple marriage creates a covenant intended to combine you, your spouse, and the Savior as one.

Familial relationships are potentially the source of our greatest joy and fulfillment in life. We recognize this but often find in them our greatest sorrows and heartaches. Most of us either married or gave birth to our biggest trial. Marriage and family is part of the refining fire. Perhaps nowhere else is there a better chance to develop our capacity to love, bless, forgive, and serve than in our own families.

One key to developing celestial relationships came to me from an unexpected source: a wilderness therapy program called the Anasazi Foundation. Anasazi takes troubled teens into the desert wilderness of Arizona for six weeks and teaches them basic survival skills, along with life principles through simple concepts in nature.[90] It is a remarkable program. Many of the young people entering this program have serious problems with drugs, immorality, or other self-destructive behaviors. Six weeks later, many emerge from their experience fundamentally changed.

What surprised me most was Anasazi's focus. Rather than addressing the specific behaviors involved, they work to help the teens have a change of heart. They speak of having a *heart at war* versus a *heart at peace*. These young people arrive with bitterness, frustration, and rage in their hearts. They feel victimized and blame others for their problems. Many hold pain from damaged relationships. Their hearts are at war.

Years ago, President Benson identified enmity as being the core of pride.[91] *Enmity* means a state of opposition, antagonism or hostility. This enmity may be directed at God or others around us. A heart filled with pride is a heart at war.

The opposite of a heart at war is a heart at peace. The Savior described Himself as meek and lowly at heart. He had a heart at peace, even during great adversity. His heart was filled with humility and charity. It showed in His "peaceable walk with the children of men" (Moroni 7:4). The good news is that we can choose how our hearts will be.

Why does our heart matter? Because, as Alma tells us, what we send out will return to us again (see Alma 41:15). If my heart is at war, it often provokes war in the hearts of others. If my heart is at peace, it invites others to have peace as well.

When we change ourselves, we invite those around us to change in response. Over time, our interactions with one another as a married couple form a sort of dance that we do over and over. If you aren't happy in your relationship, one thing you should consider is how you may have contributed to the situation. Would you like receiving back the things you send out on a daily basis? The great news is that this is something you have complete control over. There are really only three things you do control: what you think, what you say, and what you do. But in those three things lies great power for change.

Let me share an example. On one occasion, one of my teenage children made a poor choice and did something she shouldn't have done. She was a great teenager and rarely needed to be corrected. So this particular choice was not typical of her behavior. However, it upset me because it was something I had specifically told her not to do. I was hurt and angry at the situation and responded by giving her a father's blessing (meaning a stern lecture and grounding her for the next day, which was an appropriate punishment to fit the crime).

Now, to clarify a few things, I wasn't yelling at her, and nothing I said was inappropriate or incorrect. The punishment I gave was also appropriate for the behavior. However, at the time, my heart was at war and not in the right place. As a result, she became defensive and a little defiant and tried to justify her poor choice. She angrily left the room, feeling like I was being a jerk. And she was right.

Having recently learned principles from Anasazi, I asked myself the question: *Is my heart at war or is my heart at peace toward my daughter?* I realized that my heart was not in the right place. I was responding more to my hurt and anger than from an honest desire to help my daughter grow. So after giving a little time for my emotions to subside, I tried to put myself in her shoes for a few minutes. I realized there were some things in her life that were hard for her and probably influenced her choice. I went down to her room, and as I entered, I could see that there was still anger in her eyes. However, once I started to explain that I understood such-and-such a situation and some of the challenges she was facing, her heart immediately softened. She responded by stating what a dumb choice she had made and how sorry she was about it and that she was happy to be grounded.

Now, what was the difference? In both scenarios, there was a behavior that needed to be corrected, and there was an appropriate consequence. But when my heart was in the right place, it helped my daughter to learn and grow from the experience rather than resist it—and our relationship was strengthened by the process.

Virtually anything in life can be done with a heart at war or a heart at peace. Consider, for example, the heart of Captain Moroni, a man who did not desire to be a man of blood and slay his brethren the Lamanites but did so to protect his people's families, land, liberty, and freedom. Captain Moroni went to battle with a heart at peace. He showed it when he spared the defeated Lamanites and allowed them to depart with a promise of peace (see Alma 44:20).

Is there anyone in your life toward whom you have a heart at war? If so, how can you come to have a heart of peace? Our Savior stated, "He that hath the spirit of contention is not of me, but is of the devil, who is the father of contention, and he stirreth up the hearts of men to contend with anger, one with another. Behold, this is not my doctrine, to stir up the hearts of men with anger, one against another; but this is my doctrine, that such things should be done away" (3 Nephi 11:29–30). He further taught, "If ye shall come unto me, or shall desire to come unto me, and rememberest that *thy brother hath aught against thee*—go thy way unto thy brother, and first be reconciled to thy brother, and then come unto me with full purpose of heart, and I will receive you" (3 Nephi 12:23–24; emphasis added).

Despite all of this, some find themselves in relationships where abuse, addiction, or other behaviors have destroyed all love and anything desirable in the marriage. If a man or woman has been sealed in the temple and finds himself or herself in such a relationship, is he or she forever stuck? Of course not.

The "jar" of marriage may become cracked through breaking the commandments or our covenants. In some cases, Christ can and does heal these cracks. In others, the cracks result in a permanent break. I don't believe that anyone will be eternally stuck in a relationship they do not find delightful and desirable. Only those marriages that are joyful to both partners are worth permanently sealing. The work before us is to strive to make our marriages worth preserving.

It is probably not for anyone to determine or decide when a failed marriage should end other than the married partners and the Lord. There clearly are situations where the Lord honorably releases a party to such a marriage. In other situations, the Lord may require a spouse to continue to suffer, work, and struggle along for wise purposes known to Him. Perhaps the Lord knows the other spouse will eventually change and the partner who suffered so much will become in some measure a savior on Mount Zion. Such decisions should be made carefully, with prayer and direction from the Lord.

Holy Spirit of Promise

At some point, your marriage needs to produce fruit worthy of preserving. It should begin to reflect on earth the joyful associations found in heaven. The blessings and happiness expected in the next life should begin to develop here in this life. Your jar is meant to hold the fruit of the tree of life.

When we have worked, toiled, sacrificed, and grown together sufficiently as a couple, the Lord can seal the marriage by the Holy Spirit of Promise. Much has been said and written on the Holy Spirit of Promise. Some believe it is simply the presence of the Holy Ghost at the time the temple wedding takes place. That doesn't seem accurate to me. The scriptures define it as something much greater. "Wherefore, I now send upon you another Comforter, even upon you my friends, that it may abide in your hearts, even the Holy Spirit of promise. . . . This Comforter is the promise which I give unto you of eternal life, even the glory of the celestial kingdom" (D&C 88:3–4).

The Holy Spirit of Promise is the Lord's promise to you of eternal life. That isn't the same thing as the empty jar that you received on the day of your wedding. Rather, it is the Lord placing a final seal upon a marriage that has become worthy of preserving through all eternity. It is a jar filled with fruit.

Without this eventual ratifying seal of the Holy Spirit of Promise, the jar loses its value, even if the marriage originated in the temple with the expectation of it being eternal. Read this scripture carefully. "If a man marry a wife, and make a covenant with her *for time and for all eternity* [this is the expectation most have upon leaving the temple on their wedding day], if that covenant . . . is not sealed by the Holy Spirit of promise . . . *then it is not valid* neither of force when they are out of the world, because they are not joined by me, saith the Lord, neither by my word" (D&C 132:18; emphasis added). Not everyone who is married in the temple will inherit celestial glory because not everyone will live up to their obligations and covenants, so not every temple marriage will be sealed up by the Holy Spirit of Promise.

The Covenant of Marriage

In a gospel context, marriage is much greater than a social organization defined and redefined by society. When a man and a woman marry in the manner that God desires for His children, consider what comes in preparation for that event. Think about all of the gospel ordinances received prior to the temple sealing. Both the woman and the man as individuals enter into a covenant relationship with the Lord. Only then is a covenant formed between the two of them and the Lord in a new, potentially everlasting relationship. This new covenant becomes something greater than either the man or the woman alone. Your marriage is one of the few things that can possibly endure beyond this transitory world and be recognized by God in the eternities (see D&C 132:15–24).

The first chapter of this book discussed the implications of a covenant relationship with the Lord. Many of those same ideas are found in the covenant between a man and a woman in marriage. Some of the same covenant practices have carried forward in our wedding traditions. For example, in our western cultures, a wife usually takes the name of her husband. Economic assets and liabilities become shared. Strengths are combined. A husband is expected to protect and care for his wife, even to laying down his life for her. A token of the covenant is involved as wedding rings are exchanged. And though we may not have a formal covenantal meal, the idea may still be present when a bride and groom feed one another the first bites of their wedding cake in celebration at the reception.

One of the rites God intended for marriage is the sexual union of the man and the woman. Ideally, this union will bear fruit. After Adam and Eve entered into a covenant relationship, they received a command to multiply (Genesis 1:28). As part of that covenant, Adam knew his wife (Moses 5:2). Children were the fruit of his loins and her womb. These children were born into a covenant.

Covenant symbols are found throughout this rite and ordinance of marriage. Chad Clark diagrammed this imagery on his blog, as outlined on the following page.

The man (Adam) divides the woman (Eve).
Blood is shed (sometimes a part of the initial act of intercourse).
A covenant is cut (formed).
A seed divides the egg.
The two (seed and egg) become one.
The cells begin to multiply.
New life begins.
The fruit grows.
The mother labors.
The child divides the woman.
Blood is again shed (during childbirth).
A covenant is again cut.
Her labors bear fruit.[92]

Those who enter this order of the priesthood, or the new and ever-lasting covenant of marriage (see D&C 131:2), are admonished to keep all of the laws, rites, and ordinances pertaining to it. Certainly these obligations would include the commandment given to multiply and replenish (fill) the earth (see Genesis 1:27–28). This law belongs only within the covenant of marriage.

The rite (or ritual) by which we multiply is (or at least should be) a sacred and holy sexual union. In God's order, only a man and a woman joined in the covenant of marriage have the right to participate in and perform this rite. It is part of the two becoming one. It is not just a physical connection, but potentially a deeply powerful emotional and spiritual connection as well. Beyond that, it is the means whereby women and men act as partners with God in creating new life. This is why sexual sins are so serious in nature. They tamper with the powers of life. When used improperly, these sacred things that are intended as a blessing to us become instead an abomination in the sight of God (see Alma 39:5).

No wonder Satan seeks to profane and trivialize these sacred things in every way possible. We see this all around us in the world. Regardless of how others may profane them, however, we can still choose to hold them sacred in our own lives.

Which brings us to the ordinances pertaining to marriage. If one of the laws is to multiply and one of the rites is a holy sexual union, then what are the ordinances that specifically pertain to marriage? While we may not usually think of it in these terms, birth may be considered the first great ordinance of this life. It is a new *living endowment*, wherein a spirit is miraculously endowed with a physical temple or body. We need a body to receive a fulness of joy (see D&C 93:33–34). In light of this, perhaps there is no holier priesthood ordinance than the ordinance of birth.

The man and woman are given the law to multiply. Together, they participate in the rite of sexual union, or passing the seed. The woman then labors alone through pregnancy and the ordinance of physical birth in bringing forth a child. The father then blesses and formally names the chid through an ordinance. Both parents are to participate in the rearing of and caring for their offspring. And they share the responsibility to teach the child the ways of God (see D&C 68:25).

Under the gospel plan, everyone should be born twice. A spiritual birth is required to follow our physical birth. The man, as a priest, should perform the ordinance of baptism associated with this spiritual birth.

The baptism by fire and the Holy Ghost follows from Christ and flows from His atoning sacrifice. Thus, the full "ordinance" of birth is actually performed in three stages. The first step is performed by the priestess in giving birth, the second by the priest in the baptism, and the third by God Himself in bestowing the Holy Ghost.

None of the steps, however, are possible without God as the other covenant partner. His involvement is required in each part of the process, from conception through the baptism by fire and the Holy Ghost. For fruit worthy of preservation into eternity, cooperation must occur between the woman, the man, and the Lord. Each contributes to and is indispensable in this process.

The Lord taught Adam that just as we are born into the world by water, blood, and the spirit, these same elements are again present in our spiritual rebirth (see Moses 6:59). We are born of water (baptism), of the spirit (Holy Ghost), and cleansed by the blood of Christ.

This order of priesthood (or marriage) creates a godly connection between a woman, man, and God. Within this covenant are contained the laws, rites, and ordinances necessary to bring about joy to the participants and fulfill the divine purposes of God.

The Law of Chastity

In light of all this, it is no wonder that sexual relations are sacred to the Lord. When God's plan is discarded, sexual unions often result in total chaos. Participants may feel used, and children may be born unwanted, into broken homes, or not raised in an enduring covenant. Our world largely tries to define sex in terms of personal physical gratification and nothing more. The primary concern becomes avoiding any unwanted consequences from sexual activities. Thus, "safe sex" is the world's objective. Exercising restraint and discipline, waiting for marriage, chastity, and other such notions are mocked as old-fashioned and outdated.

The world's standards are loudly and effectively communicated all around us. Our youth are constantly bombarded with these counter-voices. At times, perhaps, we fail to present the Lord's standards as effectively. Our youth need to understand why sex is sacred and that they have a choice.

Jacob summarized the great battle of life in these words: "Remember, to be carnally-minded is death, and to be spiritually-minded is life eternal" (2 Nephi 9:39). What does it mean to be "carnally-minded"? Several things come to mind. For instance, when we trust in the "arm of flesh" or rely upon our own wisdom rather than God, we are being carnally-minded. Focusing on the physical side of life and ignoring the spiritual realities of our nature and the world around us is also being carnally-minded. The dictionary defines *carnal* as relating to physical, especially sexual needs, desires, and activities. In part, carnal things are related to the desires, appetites, and passions built into our physical bodies. So how does being carnally-minded lead to death, considering that our physical bodies are a great blessing?

The Prophet Joseph Smith declared, "We came to this earth that we might have a body and present it pure before God in the celestial kingdom. *The great principle of happiness consists in having a body.* The devil has no body, and herein is his punishment."[93] Satan, deprived of a body, tempts us to misuse our own.

If our physical bodies are a blessing, then what does Jacob mean? In the temple, we find an answer. There, we learn that our desires, appetites, and passions are to be kept within certain boundaries set by the Lord. It isn't that the Lord doesn't intend for us to eat or sleep or reproduce, but rather that these things are to be done in wisdom and as the Lord directs. In this way, they become blessings to us rather than challenges. Our spirits are to master our bodies—not the other way around. This is part of the challenge of mortality. Satan often approaches us through the desires, appetites, and passions of our bodies. Sometimes, he can succeed there when he can't appeal to our spirit. Most of the help we receive from the Lord in this battle comes to our spirits, whereas much of the temptation and struggle we face comes through our flesh.

This can be difficult for us to learn. As infants, we are born totally helpless. Babies only know how to respond to physical needs. As we grow, our natural man can become consumed with physical needs and desires to the exclusion of other things. This is not the Lord's way. We all must learn to live His law of chastity.

Some wonder why chastity is so important, as long as there are no unintended consequences. Others feel that if a young man and woman are deeply in love and committed to one another, then there is no need to wait for marriage. Why shouldn't they live together first to see how things work out? For some of our young men and women, these may be honest, sincere questions that deserve answers.

Alma provided one. He taught his son, "See that ye bridle all your passions, *that ye may be filled with love*" (Alma 38:12; emphasis added). Because our souls are composed of body and spirit, physical actions often have spiritual consequences. For instance, the Bible teaches that whoever commits adultery destroys his own soul (see Proverbs 6:32). Our spirits and bodies are interconnected perhaps to a greater degree than we realize. Therefore, physical choices often have spiritual effects.

Let's put Alma's words in a more modern context. In economics, we find a concept called the law of increasing and decreasing returns. It is basically the idea that there is an optimum level of input into a system to get an optimum output. Beyond that point, adding more input is wasteful and may actually be harmful. For example, if you want to grow crops, adding some fertilizer to the ground will increase your harvest. But at a certain point, adding more fertilizer will not help, and excessive amounts may even hurt the crop or destroy it.

A similar concept comes into play with respect to our physical desires. If you feel hot, tired, and hungry on a warm summer day, a big bowl of ice cream might be just the thing. A second bowl may even be good. But if you continue eating, you probably won't receive the same satisfaction from the third and fourth bowl that you did from the first. In fact, at some point, you will get so full that continuing to eat more may even make you sick. (Sadly, I know this from experience. As a kid, I once ate an entire box of ice cream and got so sick that I couldn't stand to even look at ice cream for several years afterward.)

In the culture of the drug world, this idea of diminishing returns is sometimes called *chasing the dragon*. The first time people use a drug, they may get an incredible high that can last for hours or days. Eventually, however, this high wears off and leaves users lower than before, so they return to the drug, trying to regain that high. It's never as good as the first time. To compensate, users may increase their dosage. This may work for a while, but over time the highs decrease and decrease, and the lows always return and may even worsen. The drug users end up *chasing the dragon*, always trying to return to that first high and never getting there. Eventually, they may even reach a point that their bodies need the drug just to feel normal. These things never bring lasting peace or happiness.

It can be the same with pornography or any other addictive behavior, and it can be the same with sex. Look at some people in our society. Many have admitted to sleeping with hundreds of different partners. Why wasn't one enough? What were they looking for in the hundredth partner that they couldn't have found in any of their previous ones? How much did that one additional person even mean to them? Do they even know each partner's name? Such people are also chasing an elusive dragon. How empty, hollow, and void are these casual relationships! But many in our society are following the same path and are caught up in these chains of hell.

It is easy to see why the Lord puts boundaries on these things. Our passions need to be bridled to become a blessing to us. With a horse, a bridle can give you control over a powerful animal. Without it, the horse could run off and carry you with it. As Alma taught, our passions must be bridled so we may be filled with love.

Again, we see a connection between the physical and the spiritual. Your capacity to love your spouse (or future spouse) and others and experience genuine love (as opposed to lust) is partly tied to learning to bridle your passions. How many marriages have been destroyed by one spouse's addiction to pornography? A man or woman's serious addiction, if left unchecked, can eventually destroy a person's ability to truly love his or her spouse, and in some cases it may even prevent a normal sexual relationship.

On the other side of the coin, within the Lord's boundaries, we can find increasing returns. Within the covenant of marriage, sex can create a loving bond between a husband and wife. This bond isn't just physical. It is also emotional and spiritual, and it was meant to be so. At the right time and place, it is a wonderful part of the love and life and intimacy intended to be shared in a marriage. It is part of an eternal covenant. It was never meant to be a shack-up-and-wait-for-someone-better-to-come-along situation.

Over time, the love and relationship between spouses is intended to grow. It requires nurturing, work, and sacrifice. But as the bonds develop and deepen, so does the joy and satisfaction from the relationship. Rather than diminishing, the returns grow. They become real and lasting, even eternal, rather than fleeting and temporary. They fill you rather than empty your soul.

As I write this, my wife and I have been married for twenty-seven years. I honestly love her more today than I did on the day we were married. Yes, we have had ups and downs and struggles and have had to work at it, but it has become a source of great and profound joy for both of us. We wouldn't trade our marriage for anything. This only comes about as both partners are true and faithful to God and one another. Don't be distracted by the temptations and lies Satan continually throws in your path.

Sometimes, young people feel that as long as they don't cross the line, they can get close to the edge and still be okay. This is profoundly naïve. The trick for all of us is to stay far away from the line and not get close. None of us are as strong as we think. In the wrong situations, it is incredibly easy to slip off the edge.

Christ set a clear standard for just how far away from the line we should remain. He said, "Behold, it is written by them of old time, that thou shalt not commit adultery; but I say unto you, that whosoever looketh on a woman, to lust after her, hath committed adultery already in his heart. Behold, I give unto you a commandment, that ye suffer none of these things to enter into your heart" (3 Nephi 12:27–29). There's the line. Don't even let the wrong things into your heart. Stay faithful to God and to your current (or future) spouse by keeping your heart true. Then you will be able to truly give and receive love.

To the Lord, our physical bodies, marriage, and sexuality are sacred. The world profanes these things in every possible way. We all have a choice in our own lives. Will we hold them sacred or will we join the world in profaning them? As Jacob reminds us, eternal consequences rest in the balance.

In some ways, perhaps, we do a better job of teaching the don'ts than teaching the dos to our youth. As a result, some enter marriage with unrealistic expectations or beliefs. We don't always teach of the blessings sex can bring in a loving, committed marital relationship.

Our young men need to understand the need for absolute physical and emotional fidelity to their spouse. This should begin in their youth. My son-in-law decided as a young man that his wife would be the first girl he ever kissed. He kept that goal. I have no concern about him being faithful to my daughter in the future because of the great habits he formed while growing up. Growing up, he probably had no idea how special it would make her feel that he waited for her. (On the other hand, as a young man, I was more of the philosophy that no one wants to marry a bad kisser, so I got some practice.)

Regardless of our pasts, we all need to be absolutely true to our spouses in all ways and at all times. There is no room for emotional or physical infidelity in our marriages. Pornography has become an insidious infestation, destroying countless lives and families in our day. We must shun it in all its forms. We also need to be affectionate, tender, and respectful of our spouses. Sensitivity to their needs and desires and feelings can go a long way in building successful marriage relationships.

At the same time, young men and women need to understand that sex is an important part of marital intimacy. Going many days or weeks without that connection can be hard on a relationship. Women tend to have an extended support network that includes friends, family, and others in addition to their spouse. Men generally don't. For many men, their emotional and physical intimacy and support comes primarily from their wives. Men may have casual friends, but they generally only share their entire heart and feelings with a wife. Sexual intimacy is an important part of the bond for both spouses. When intimacy is withheld or absent in a marriage, one or both partners may be left feeling isolated and alone.

In our home, we have a wood stove. On a cold winter evening, nothing feels better than the heat from a fire. I often used our stove as an analogy to teach our children about sexual relationships. I asked them why we didn't just build the fire in the middle of the family room. In the wrong time, wrong place, or with the wrong person, these things can cause great damage in our lives, just like building a fire in the middle of the room. But at the right time and in the right way, then, like the stove, these relations can be a great blessing.

We need to give our children and youth a clear understanding of the Lord's standards. They also deserve an explanation of why those standards are important and how they protect us. They need to understand the dos as well as the don'ts so that they have healthy attitudes toward human sexuality and don't grow up viewing it as a "necessary evil."

And along with all of that, we must also teach sensitivity to and compassion for those who are victims of abuse and those who have made mistakes. The old adage of the chewed-up gum, taught by well-meaning youth leaders, is an affront to the Atonement and the scriptures, which teach that even big, scarlet sins can be made as white as snow (see Isaiah 1:18). Given that the law of chastity is something we all must grapple with in our lives, given that Satan's counter messages are presented daily in our culture, and given that sexuality can be a problem area in marriage, we need to do a better job of teaching our children and youth.

Homework

1. Study "Covenant Marriage" by Bruce C. Hafen (*Ensign*, October 1996).

CHAPTER 6

Application in Your Life

"And I looked, and behold a white cloud, and upon the cloud one sat like unto the Son of man, having on his head a golden crown, and in his hand a sharp sickle.

"And another angel came out of the temple, crying with a loud voice to him that sat on the cloud, Thrust in thy sickle, and reap: for the time is come for thee to reap; for the harvest of the earth is ripe.

"And he that sat on the cloud thrust in his sickle on the earth; and the earth was reaped."

—Revelation 14:14–16

A few years ago, I served as a teacher's quorum advisor. Our quorum had an annual tradition each July of climbing Utah's Mount Timpanogos. The summit sits at 11,752 feet above sea level (3,582 meters). It is a rigorous hike to reach the peak. After resting and enjoying lunch at the top, we would continue around the face of the mountain to reach the snowfield on the back side. While, technically, this permanent snowfield is not a glacier, for a bunch of eager scouts on a hot summer day, it was close enough. The scouts whooped and hollered as they sat and slid down the steep, snowy slope for a quarter mile or longer, eventually ending up at the crystal clear, icy waters of Emerald Lake. On a dare, some would inevitably take a quick polar plunge in the ice-filled water before heading back down the mountain.

Many of the young men had reservations about making the climb for the first time. It seemed a daunting challenge. One boy in particular stands out in my memory. He complained about getting up at five a.m., and then he complained it was too cold as we started hiking. The trail was too steep and too dusty. Later, it was too hot and too hard. He found one thing after another to whine about most of the way up the mountain. Some of the other boys begged us leaders to make him stop.

About four hours into the hike, the climb reaches a point called the Saddle, where it is possible to see down the front of the mountain to the valley stretched out far below. The view is spectacular. This young man finally arrived at the Saddle. For the first time that day, he stopped talking and stood silently as he took in the view. He seemed to sense just how far he had climbed. After several minutes of absolute quiet, he finally said, "Wow! That is the most amazing thing I've ever seen." Though he was exhausted and sore by the time we returned home, the accomplishment of reaching the summit was a milestone in his early life that he wouldn't forget.

Why do the scriptures sometimes compare the temple to a mountain? What lessons can we learn from that analogy? More important, where are we in our individual ascent? Are we climbing? Have we wandered off the mountain, lost the path, or stalled in our progress?

If a mountain symbolizes the Lord's house, where is the path leading us? Remember President McKay's testimony of the summit, as quoted at the start of chapter three: "Seen for what it is, it is the step-by-step ascent into the Eternal Presence." We don't reach the summit by simply attending once to receive our own ordinances. Such an idea is nonsensical. This is one reason it is such a blessing to be able to return often and serve our deceased ancestors. "For we without them cannot be made perfect; neither can they without us be made perfect" (D&C 128:18).

How do we climb this mountain? "Who shall ascend into the hill of the Lord? Or who shall stand in his holy place? He that hath clean hands, and a pure heart" (Psalm 24:3–4). It is possible to make the ascent. It requires diligent and thoughtful effort, but it is possible. Our ascent doesn't occur in a day, but it can occur in our day-to-day lives.

At times in our journey, we may need to stop to rest and catch our breath. We may even take a lunch break or reach a plateau that delays us for a time. But let us not lose sight of the summit and where the climb is taking us. The temple is intended to return us to the presence of our Savior. The view from there is beyond anything in this world. "Eye hath not seen, nor ear heard, neither have entered into the heart of man, the things which God hath prepared for them that love him" (1 Corinthians 2:9).

A view of these things is promised to all who seek it.

> Great and marvelous are the works of the Lord, and the mysteries of his kingdom which he showed unto us, which surpass all understanding in glory, and in might, and in dominion; which he commanded us we should not write while we were yet in the Spirit, and are not lawful for man to utter; neither is man capable to make them known, for they are only to be seen and understood by the power of the Holy Spirit, which God bestows on those who love him, and purify themselves before him; *to whom he grants this privilege of seeing and knowing for themselves.* (D&C 76:114–17; emphasis added)

Whether we receive this privilege or not is largely our choice. God is willing for all to receive these things.

Joseph Smith testified, "Reading the experience of others, or the revelation given to *them*, can never give *us* a comprehensive view of our condition and true relation to God. Knowledge of these things can only be obtained by experience through the ordinances of God set forth for that purpose. Could you gaze into heaven five minutes, you would know more than you would by reading all that ever was written on the subject."[94]

Learning by Study and by Faith

The gospel is meant to unfold line upon line. It is a process that takes time. We must be patient but diligent. In many ways, we are no different from Adam. He received a commandment to offer sacrifices as part of his worship, but no explanation was provided (see Moses 5:5). Nevertheless, Adam obeyed. It was many days (perhaps years or even decades) later that an angel appeared and taught him the meaning of his sacrifices (see Moses 5:6–8). The Lord has purpose in His timing. We are tested and tried along the way.

In like manner, we may attend the temple often without fully understanding everything. And yet we are not meant to remain in ignorance. We are commanded to seek learning by study and by faith. In the dedicatory prayer of the Kirtland Temple, we read, "And do thou grant, Holy Father, that all those who shall worship in this house may be taught words of wisdom out of the best books, and that they may seek learning even by study, and also by faith. . . . And that they may grow up in thee, and receive a fulness of the Holy Ghost" (D&C 109:14–15). The Lord does not want us to remain in ignorance.

We should study the temple and our covenants. Certainly the best books on these subjects are the scriptures. The Lord has messages for us in the scriptures and in the temple ceremony that we have not yet received. We are given more only as we give diligent heed to that which we have already received.

So much of our scripture is related to the temple. Once we begin to look, we encounter temple themes over and over again in the scriptures. Even something as familiar as the story of Jonah and the whale encompasses temple themes. Jonah's story is one of a fall and redemption. At the lowest point in his life, which he describes as the "belly of hell," Jonah pondered on and looked toward the temple (see Jonah 2:2, 4, 7). He concluded, "I will pay that that I have vowed. Salvation is of the Lord" (Jonah 2:9). Jonah resolved to keep his covenants.

In addition to our study, we are also commanded to seek learning by faith. Learning by faith involves receiving personal revelation. It is being taught by heaven. Joseph Smith instructed, "The best way to obtain truth and wisdom is not to ask it from books, but to go to God in prayer, and obtain divine teaching."[95] There are some things we simply cannot learn from books, including the scriptures. These things we need to learn directly from God.

For example, the scriptures teach that each of us has a spiritual gift or gifts from God. Do you know what your gift is and how God would have you use it to bless those around you? How can you discover that without revelation? What things were you foreordained to accomplish in your life? What is your current standing before the Lord? What would He have you do with your life? Answers to these kinds of questions generally come only through revelation. To fully grow as God intends, we must develop faith and increase in our ability to receive personal revelation.

Developing Your Faith

The Lord has declared, "I work not among the children of men save it be according to their faith" (2 Nephi 27:23). This is a sobering statement. God doesn't work in our lives unless we have faith. If we don't readily see God's hand in our lives, it should give us cause to seriously examine our personal faith.

We cannot progress along the path outlined in the temple endowment without faith. Moving from one step or level to the next requires us to exercise faith. This raises the question, what exactly is faith? How does one obtain it? How does it grow? Maybe we understand faith intuitively better than we can put into words.

The scriptures teach that faith comes by hearing the word of God (see Romans 10:17) and that the word of God is vital to helping it grow (see Alma 32:22–23, 26–43). Have you ever stopped to wonder why? It is because our faith must be based upon truth to be of effect. If we have faith in false beliefs, our faith will not yield the desired fruit. The scriptures refer to this problem as *unbelief*. No matter how firmly and fervently one holds to false beliefs, they will avail nothing. For faith to be effective, it must be based on truth. We need the undiluted word of God in our lives from true messengers sent from God. Saving faith cannot be built upon the philosophies of men, even when mingled with scriptures.

Initially, the word of God comes to us from outside sources, such as the scriptures or by the testimonies of missionaries. But could the scriptural phrase *hearing the word of God* also include God speaking directly with us? Is there a better way to receive His word? While faith may indeed begin by hearing the word of God preached through an authorized messenger, eventually our faith should include and be founded upon our own personal and unique experiences with the Lord God.

The book of Enos is not included in the Book of Mormon simply to tell us about Enos's experience. Rather, it stands as an invitation for us to reach up, like Enos, and have our own encounter with God. Enos is a model. His faith began by being taught the word of God by his father. He recalled, "The words which I had often heard my father speak concerning eternal life, and the joy of the saints, sunk deep into my heart" (Enos 1:3). Though his father's words contained truth and provided a basis for his faith, still they could not tell Enos of his own standing before God. That knowledge had to come from Him.

Enos recorded the result of his father's teachings and the concern he had about his own spiritual standing. He stated, "My soul hungered" (Enos 1:4). He had been taught about eternal life and the joy of the Saints. Enos believed his father's testimony. He recognized that hearing about these things and having faith in them was not the same thing as possessing them for himself. So his soul hungered for them, to the point that he knelt before his Maker and cried unto Him in mighty prayer, until his voice reached the heavens and he received a reply (see Enos 1:4–5).

Enos then knew for himself. His faith was subsequently based upon the word of God directly to himself and not solely upon his father's testimony. We are invited to do the same. How many members of the Church today have faith in the Restoration, try to live the gospel, labor and serve diligently in their callings, and yet feel uncertain as to their individual standing before the Lord? If you are uncertain, how else can you know unless you go to the Lord as did Enos?

A stake president I know likes to remind his stake that our faith is to be centered in Christ and not in a particular outcome. There is wisdom in that reminder. Some who place their faith in a particular outcome—being healed of an illness, for example—may find their faith shaken if that desired outcome is not realized. Our faith should be centered in Christ. However, when we obtain a promise directly from God, we should have absolute faith in its eventual fulfillment.

God's promises may not always be realized in exactly the way we anticipate or expect. Blessings also occur on God's timetable, not on our own. But we are assured that his word will always be fulfilled. In the interim period between receiving God's promise and seeing its fulfillment, we have hope. Gospel hope is not a flimsy thing, like buying a lottery ticket and hoping to make a fortune. It is based upon God's word to us and is a result of our faith. "For without faith there cannot be any hope" (Moroni 7:42). Unless we approach God in faith, we cannot receive His word and promises. We then are left in our uncertainty, without firm hope.

The answers that come from God often require us to take action. For example, an investigator may pray to know if the Book of Mormon is true. The answer to that prayer is not usually seen or observable to an outside person; however, receiving the answer may require the investigator to accept baptism in faith. This action (baptism) is the physical, concrete evidence of the unseen answer to the prayer of faith. This is why faith is also defined as the evidence of things not seen (see Hebrews 11:1). We receive spiritual and unseen communications from God and bring these by our actions into the concrete, physical reality of our day-to-day lives. These actions are evidence of the unseen communications from the Lord.

Most simply, faith is belief put into action. This is why James taught that faith without works is dead, and why he declared, "I will shew thee my faith by my works" (see James 2:17–18, 26.) Faith then is a principle of action.[96] It is also a principle of power, because as we act in faith, it permits God to invoke His power. Without faith, God's hand is not visible among men (see 2 Nephi 27:23).

Perhaps we should regularly take time to evaluate our own level of faith. Is God at work in your life as a result of your faith? Mormon provides us with a measuring stick. He wrote, "It is by faith that miracles are wrought; and it is by faith that angels appear and minister unto men; wherefore, if these things have ceased wo be unto the children of men, for it is because of unbelief, and all is vain. For no man can be saved, according to the words of Christ, save they shall have faith in his name; wherefore, *if these things have ceased, then has faith ceased also*; and awful is the state of man, for they are as though there had been no redemption made" (Moroni 7:37–38). Once again, the Book of Mormon hits us with a sobering message.

Regardless of how active or involved we may see ourselves in the Church or how much service or good we think we are doing, unless we are seeing miracles and the Lord's hand at work in our lives, then, according to Mormon, we don't have faith, and it is because of unbelief. That is a startling statement—one that should give us pause for serious internal reflection. It might be painful to admit to ourselves that we perhaps don't have as much faith as we'd like to believe. But that realization can provide the moment, like Enos, that causes our souls to hunger for something more.

Religion isn't just a bunch of rules and regulations governing our external behavior as much as it is about our experience and relationship with God and the condition of our hearts. Are your daily, weekly, and monthly private and public religious practices helping you to know God? Are you seeing the Lord's hand in your life? If not, then perhaps it is because of unbelief. What erroneous beliefs do you hold onto with respect to yourself, God, or His work in your life?

Unbelief comprises a large spectrum from outright disbelief to firmly held belief in incorrect traditions or principles. And we are warned in the scriptures that the wicked one "taketh away light and truth, through disobedience . . . and because of *the tradition of their fathers*" (D&C 93:39; emphasis added). It may be difficult to unlearn things we learned in our youth that are incorrect, especially when these things are deeply ingrained in our thoughts. In some cases, our unbelief may be as simple as the feeling that we'll never be good enough or that we have to reach a certain level of "righteousness" before Christ's Atonement can work in our lives. But to whatever extent we believe things that aren't true, we suffer from unbelief. We may need to humbly ask the Lord to help us replace our unbelief with belief.

We often hear that fear is the opposite of faith. And the scriptures command us to doubt not and fear not (see, for example, Doctrine and Covenants 6:36). That is easier said than done. It is not always easy to set aside fears and doubts. Examining our fears can be helpful, revealing where we least trust God in our lives.[97] In other words, what we fear most shows where we don't trust God. My greatest fear for many years was that I wasn't good enough. Essentially, I was trying to save *myself* rather than allowing Christ to save me. What are your fears? How could you go about letting them go and exercise greater faith and trust in God?

And as if all of this weren't hard enough, we are told that our faith will also be tried. Opposition is necessary for our growth. The answers to our prayers are often quiet and subtle. It may require faith to accept them and act upon them. Often, it is only after we have taken a step or two into the dark that things become clear. That step is critical, though, because it is by doing that we gain understanding (see John 7:17).

In other words, God's initial answer to us is often incomplete. It may not make complete sense. Yet, if we will act in faith and move forward, we will come to know and understand more. Adam would not have been taught by the angel if he had not first observed the command to offer sacrifices. Initially, offering sacrifice was an act of faith. Later, he acquired knowledge. Acting in faith is required for learning by faith.

There is a process we often go through as our faith develops. Recognizing this cycle can help us endure the opposition we will face. It is diagrammed below.

How Faith Grows – Faith Cycle

The cycle often begins with a question or some confusion or doubt in our minds. We take our question to the Lord in faith and receive an answer from Him. Then we act upon the answer, walking forward in faith in response to the direction we received. Sometimes everything falls into place. Often, however, we encounter opposition. Things don't go as expected and may even be so bad that failure seems unavoidable.

There can be a real temptation during this opposition to look back and question the original answer from God. It is easy to second-guess ourselves and wonder why things aren't working out. We may even want to give up or change directions. However, we should not lose faith in God's original answer.

Satan also steps in to plant seeds of doubt. He often tries to get us to question God's word to us. When he approached Adam and Eve, he directly contradicted God's words to them, telling them they would not die if they ate the fruit (see Genesis 3:2–5). Likewise, right after the Father declared to Christ that He was His Beloved Son (see Matthew 3:17), Satan came to whisper doubt: "If thou be the Son of God, command that these stones be made bread" (see Matthew 4:3–6). We can be sure he will try to get us to doubt the words God gives us as well.

It is vital at this point to heed Paul's counsel to not cast away our confidence (see Hebrews 10:35). Elder Holland gave an excellent talk on this subject. In it, he stated, "Beware the temptation to retreat from a good thing. If it was right when you prayed about it and trusted it and lived for it, it is right now."[98]

We must press forward through the opposition, even when it persists over time. Sometimes, things may get so bad that it appears failure is imminent. The Lord may wait until this moment to intervene. But He does intercede, and miracles do occur. We see the hand of the Lord revealed, and our faith and trust and confidence in Him grows. We move forward with increased faith. Eventually, however, the cycle will repeat in our lives. All of these experiences are designed to help our faith grow and increase our trust and confidence in God.

We see an example of this faith cycle in the life of Joseph Smith. He questioned which church to join and studied it out in the Bible, seeking an answer. He encountered the verse in James giving him the direction he needed. He pondered this answer and moved forward in faith, only to encounter Satan's opposition as he began to pray. The opposition continued until Joseph was ready to give up and accept destruction. At that moment, he was delivered, and the miracle occurred (see Joseph Smith—History 1:11–17).

Another example is found in the story of the brass plates. Nephi accepted the commandment to return to Jerusalem for the plates and moved forward in the faith that God would open a way to accomplish it. But he and his brothers failed twice. In the second attempt, they barely managed to escape with their lives. There was no indication that the Lord was with them. His brothers, angry at the loss of their wealth, beat Nephi until the angel of the Lord intervened (see 1 Nephi 3:29). It was not until this moment of apparent failure that the Lord's hand was revealed.[99] The angel promised that if they returned, the Lord would deliver Laban into their hands.

Even after the angel departed, his brothers continued to murmur. Nephi admonished them to be faithful by reminding them of the experience of Moses and the Red Sea (see 1 Nephi 4:1–2). This provides us with a glimpse into how Nephi could persevere through the opposition. He recognized that Moses and the ancient Israelites were led through the same cycle. He knew that God supported them and that, in like manner, God would support him as well.

Young missionaries often experience the same cycle in our day. They might wonder whether they should serve a mission and may receive a witness from God that they are to serve. Acting in faith upon that answer, they accept a call, only to enter the mission field to find they can't seem to learn the language or can't stand their companion, or can't find anyone interested in their message. Weeks or even months of struggle may ensue. But as these missionaries attest, eventually the miracles follow.

It should not be a surprise that each of us goes through the same process in developing our own faith. Recognizing the cycle can make it easier to patiently work through the opposition we all encounter.

Faith is crucial to our salvation. As the *Lectures on Faith* teach, in order for our faith to be effective, we must know that the path we are pursuing through life is according to God's will.[100] The big picture, or overall view of that path, is outlined in the temple endowment. It requires continuing faith to move along the path. But it also requires revelation from God to implement and adapt the specifics of the path to our individual lives. Without receiving personal revelation, our faith can never become perfect and fruitful.

Growing in the Principle of Revelation

Learning by faith necessarily involves receiving revelation. We must connect with and be taught by heaven. We cannot learn everything we need to accomplish the Lord's will in our lives without personal revelation. As the endowment testifies, we must approach the Lord.

Joseph Smith declared, "Salvation cannot come without revelation; it is vain for anyone to minister without it."[101] We cannot be saved without receiving personal revelation. We cannot effectively minister in our families and in our Church callings without revelation to guide and assist us. How can we possibly do the Lord's will if we do not know it? The Holy Ghost is given to "show unto you all things what ye should do" (2 Nephi 32:5).

We cannot learn everything we need to know in a sacrament meeting or a stake conference or even in general conference. The Lord desires each of us to know Him, which is eternal life (see John 17:3). Knowing Him is not the same thing as knowing *about* Him. He wants to have a relationship with us. We are to *follow Him*. The temple testifies plainly of these truths.

Joseph Smith warned the early Saints about depending too heavily upon their leaders and not standing on their own feet. Doing so, he said, was "neglecting the duties devolving upon themselves."[102] These early Saints made the same mistake ancient Israel had made with Moses (see Exodus 20:19–21). They wanted Joseph to speak to the Lord for them instead of learning to obtain revelation and answers for themselves. Joseph warned them against this. He didn't want them developing the attitude that everything they needed to know the Lord would tell them through the prophet. While we should sustain and support our leaders, we cannot abdicate our personal responsibility to receive revelation in our individual lives. Otherwise, we neglect the blessings and obligations of the gospel.

So how do we do it? How do we grow in our ability to receive personal revelation? Once again, Nephi provides us with an answer. He stated, "Do ye not remember the things which the Lord hath said?— If ye will not harden your hearts, and ask me in faith, believing that ye shall receive, with diligence in keeping my commandments, surely these things shall be made known unto you" (1 Nephi 15:11). In this one verse, we find three keys to revelation:

- Ask in faith
- Believe God will answer
- Diligently keep His commandments

Let's consider each of these keys individually.

First, ask in faith. We know that we receive blessings from God by obedience to the law upon which the blessings are predicated (see D&C 130:21). Asking is one of those laws. There are certain blessings available that we simply cannot receive without asking and seeking for. This is why the scriptures repeatedly admonish: "Ask, and it shall be given unto you; seek, and ye shall find; knock, and it shall be opened unto you" (3 Nephi 14:7). Asking, seeking, and knocking are keys! I believe the opposite is also true. Some doors will never open unless you ask, seek, and knock.

The endowment testifies plainly of this process. The ceremony concludes with us asking for and receiving further knowledge. The Doctrine and Covenants also plainly testifies, "*If thou shalt ask*, thou shalt receive revelation upon revelation, knowledge upon knowledge, that thou mayest know the mysteries and peaceable things—that which bringeth joy, that which bringeth life eternal" (D&C 42:61; emphasis added). If you don't ask, you're not going to receive. There are many good men and women who live righteous lives but who receive less than they could receive simply because they do not ask, seek, and knock in faith.

Consider Joseph Smith's life. The entire Restoration started with Joseph's going to God in prayer with a question. Several years then passed before Joseph once again went to God, seeking forgiveness and wishing to know his standing before the Lord. This resulted in Moroni's visit and Joseph's call to translate the Book of Mormon. Nearly every revelation contained in the Doctrine and Covenants came as a result of Joseph going to the Lord with a question. That pattern should tell us something about how God will work in our lives as well.

We find the same thing in the life of the brother of Jared. He received great promises and revelations from the Lord, who then told him, "thus I will do unto thee *because this long time ye have cried unto me*" (Ether 1:43; emphasis added).

What would have happened if Joseph and the brother of Jared had not approached the Lord in prayer? How different would their lives have been? What blessings is the Lord waiting to give us if we will but cry unto Him? We must approach the Lord in faith; otherwise, nothing happens. He waits patiently for us. God does no work until there is faith present. Do you suppose there are things God is waiting to tell you? If your faith has become stagnant, then begin to exercise it.

The second key is to have faith that God will answer. This belief may be tentative at the beginning. Like the uncertain prayer of the Lamanite king, "O God . . . *if there is a God, and if thou art God*, wilt thou make thyself known unto me, and I will give away all my sins to know thee" (see Alma 22:18; emphasis added). This king was not even sure if there really was someone out there, but God honored his plea because of his sincerity and willingness to respond to God's answer.

Contrast his response with that of Laman and Lemuel. When Nephi asked if they had inquired of the Lord, they responded, "We have not; for the Lord maketh no such thing known unto us" (1 Nephi 15:9). God would have answered them if they had inquired, but they did not, and thus their words became self-fulfilling prophecy. God wants to talk with each of us, but often He waits until we seek Him in humility and sincerity.

Receiving answers requires us to listen and watch for the answers. It may also mean some work, study, and effort on our part. As Oliver Cowdery learned, it is not enough to simply ask without taking any further thought (see D&C 9:7). Joseph Smith labored over the scriptures with his question about which church he should join for some time before he went to the Lord in prayer.

The third key is to diligently keep God's commandments. There is no reason for the Lord to give us more when we are not living up to what we have already received. Often, God's answers to our prayers require further action on our part. If we do not do as He directs, then we shouldn't expect continued guidance.

Part of truly learning involves doing and becoming. We receive light and truth as we keep the commandments (see D&C 93:28). And then conversely, we lose light and truth through disobedience (see D&C 93:39). Christ taught that only when we do shall we truly know (see John 7:17). Our diligence and obedience are absolutely necessary to gain the kind of knowledge that saves. But notice it is obedience to the Lord's commandments.

Many Jews at the time of Christ took their obedience to an extreme, adding to and going beyond what the Lord had commanded. In their rigid attempts to keep the Sabbath day holy, they piled on rules and regulations. They then judged and criticized Christ for healing on the Sabbath. The irony of their extreme and rigid form of obedience is that they rejected the God who gave them the commandments in the first place. We must avoid falling into the same trap.

Is obedience ultimately about exact, rigid adherence to the *For the Strength of Youth* pamphlet, a university honor code, mission rules, or some other set of standards? Or is it something more? (I'm not suggesting we scrap our standards! They are important. But I am hoping that we will pause to think about them and their purpose in our lives and the principles behind them.)

Consider the Savior's perfect obedience. Of His life, He stated, "Behold I have given unto you my gospel, and this is the gospel which I have given unto you—that I came into the world to do the will of my Father, because my Father sent me" (3 Nephi 27:13). That is the essence! *Our Savior's obedience was perfect because He never varied from His Father's will.* We must seek to do the same. When we get an answer or direction from the Lord, we need to accept and follow it, regardless of the cost or consequences. That is true obedience.

This is a lesson Nephi learned early in his life. Whatever God requires is right, no matter what it is. This is why we too must be "led by the spirit" (1 Nephi 4:6), not always knowing beforehand the things we should do. I'm pretty certain that killing Laban would violate the *For the Strength of Youth* standards. And yet, Nephi encountered this dilemma early in his journey.

The Lord could have made it easy. Laban could have suffered a heart attack or any number of other complications that would have resulted in Nephi's finding Laban already dead in the streets of Jerusalem. But He did not. He used the situation to test and teach Nephi. Nephi recorded it for our benefit.

Joseph Smith taught the early Saints,

Happiness is the object and design of our existence; and will be the end
thereof, if we pursue the path that leads to it; and this path is virtue,
uprightness, faithfulness, holiness, and keeping all the commandments of God. But we cannot keep all the commandments without
first knowing them, and we cannot expect to know all, or more than
we now know unless we comply with or keep those we have already
received. That which is wrong under one circumstance, may be, and
often is, right under another.

God said, "Thou shalt not kill"; at another time He said, "Thou
shalt utterly destroy." This is the principle on which the government of
heaven is conducted—by revelation adapted to the circumstances in
which the children of the kingdom are placed. *Whatever God requires is
right, no matter what it is,* although we may not see the reason thereof
till long after the events transpire.[103]

A few years ago, while working in the temple, I was helping a
young man who had come to receive his endowment before leaving
to serve a mission. His mother had died when he was about twelve
years old, and he had been raised by his father, who remained a wid-
ower. He and his father were at the temple together. I was prompted
by the Spirit to share a scripture with him. In hindsight, I believe the
Lord (and possibly his mother) wanted him to have that scripture in
his heart as he embarked on his mission. Despite the persistence of
the prompting, I didn't follow it because it was against the rules we
have as ordinance workers. I obeyed the *rules* but didn't obey God.
I have regretted it ever since. I missed an opportunity to bless that
young man's life in a way that the Lord wanted him to be blessed. I
resolved then to never ignore direction from the Spirit, no matter how
difficult or inconvenient to me.

I learned something else from this experience. One of the reasons
we may argue with or ignore the promptings we receive is because
they require us to do something we aren't planning to do or may not
want to do. And that makes sense. If we were going to do something
anyway, the Lord has no need to prompt us to do it.

It is helpful to recognize that many of the promptings you will
receive will be for something you aren't planning to do. Do them

anyway, even if you don't want to, or even if obeying requires you to violate a rule or a commandment. In that case, make certain, however, that it is really coming from the Spirit. People sometimes use this principle to justify their own sinful desires or bad behavior. You know when you are right with the Lord and doing His will and when you are not.

Obedience is seeking to do the Lord's will above all else, regardless of the personal cost. We should all seek that. And, as in all things, the Savior is our perfect example.

Receiving Answers

Receiving answers to prayer is a deeply personal and subjective process. I have had many answers and many experiences. I can't prove them to you or anyone else. But that doesn't change the fact that they happened. You probably have had many of your own. God wants to talk with us.

In recent years, I have found that the Lord is much more anxious and willing to talk with me than I ever would have believed when I was younger. It was my own unbelief, lack of effort, and failure to listen that limited Him. I've been trying to correct that in my life. In the book of Helaman, we learn that Nephi and Lehi received many revelations daily (see Helaman 11:23). What a great thing for us to strive for in our own lives. The Lord is much more willing to speak with us than we generally believe.

When God first takes us by the hand and begins to walk with us, it usually begins with the simple rather than with the dramatic. It may even require some faith to accept that an answer has indeed come from Him. There is not one set way for everyone. Our experiences may be slightly different from one another's because we are unique individuals. In general, however, our first answers to prayer will come through our feelings. It started there for Oliver Cowdery. Remember, he prayed to know if the work was of God and testified that the Lord spoke peace to his soul (see D&C 6:23). When God's peace comes to you, it will be unmistakable.

For many years, this was often how I received answers. I learned to discern the feeling I had when the Spirit confirmed a decision and the feeling I had when the answer was a stupor of thought. I acted based upon those feelings, but revelation isn't intended to begin and end there.

Long before Nephi experienced his vision, he testified that the word of the Lord came to him (see 1 Nephi 2:18–19) and gave specific promises. Nephi was *hearing* the word of God. In like manner, our ability to receive revelation must also eventually move beyond feelings to include information, intelligence, words, thoughts, ideas, and messages. The word of the Lord will come to us as well. This voice is heard in your mind and heart more often than as an actual audible voice.

At times, His voice is loud and clear. I think the Lord had to yell at me a few times before I started to listen. But in my experience, more often the Lord's voice is quiet and subtle, and we have to listen for it. It may require some time and experience to learn to distinguish it from our own thoughts, but this still, small voice is probably the most common form of revelation.

Often the thoughts and ideas communicated by the voice are well beyond our own knowledge and may contain ideas or thoughts we have not considered. The Lord may also bring scriptures to our minds that contain the answers we seek. Many times, the Lord answers me in part with another question, which then requires additional thought and inquiry on my part to eventually reach a more complete answer. As we become more adept at listening, it even becomes possible to carry on lengthy conversations with the Lord in this manner.

The Lord told Oliver, "Yea, behold, I will tell you in your mind and in your heart, by the Holy Ghost, which shall come upon you and which shall dwell in your heart. Now, behold, this is the spirit of revelation; behold, this is the spirit by which Moses brought the children of Israel through the Red Sea on dry ground" (D&C 8:2–3). Despite the burning bush and other miracles wrought by the Lord, much of the revelation Moses received came through the still, small voice of the Holy Ghost.

At the same time, we should not expect that personal revelation is meant to be limited to or only include the still, small voice. Beyond the whisperings of the Holy Ghost, revelations can also come through visions, dreams, ministering angels, and so on. These may be less common but are still real. People sometimes fear these sources of revelation because of those who have been misled by them. But being deceived can happen with any form of revelation. We all must learn to distinguish between that which comes from God and that which comes from other sources.

There aren't hard-and-fast rules on how the Lord communicates with His children. He is free to do and answer as He sees fit. The way you receive answers will probably be different from how I receive them. In general, however, we likely won't experience the more miraculous forms of revelation unless—and until—we become adept at the more common, ordinary ones. There seems to be a progression as our relationship with the Lord matures and develops.

So why are there times when we do not receive an answer? Why does God sometimes remain silent? Even Joseph Smith experienced times in his life when he was left to muddle along as best he could and was unable to get answers.

Perhaps there are several reasons for this. It may be that we already have the answer but won't accept it. Or it could be that we need to make a decision first and ask if our decision is right. Or sometimes we have to choose and begin walking forward in faith. The Lord permits us to struggle and grow through the process.

Timing is another critical factor. The Lord's time frame is not always the same as ours. We may need more patience, recognizing that the answer is coming. In some cases, we may not be prepared for the answer. The Lord may send experiences to prepare us. Some requests may take years or even decades for everything to be in place and for the Lord to fully answer. Asking is critical, even in these instances. Our asking permits the Lord to set things in motion in response to our petition.

At other times, God's silence is simply part of the testing process we are all subject to. We receive no witness until after the trial of our faith (see Ether 12:6). I have experienced seasons of rich association with the Spirit and many revelations, and then other times when the Spirit seems to depart, even for an extended period, and I am left to press along on the best I can.

I really like the image Isaiah used in comparing our righteousness to the "waves of the sea" (1 Nephi 20:18). Waves ebb and flow constantly. The tides also exert their pull. Yet through it all, waves are relentless. They continue to pound away without ceasing. Our determination to follow the Lord should be the same. Though we may experience some natural ebb and flow in our lives, may we always be relentless in coming back.

Avoiding Deception

The growth we need requires effort over time. Along the way, we encounter opposition. Satan and his forces are allowed their influence. Christ had to ascend above all things and descend below all things. Satan sought to mislead and turn Him from His mission. We too will encounter both. The endowment teaches that it is necessary for us to learn to distinguish the true from the false.

I believe the thoughts in our minds can be our own, from God, or suggestions from the adversary. We need to learn to distinguish and recognize them and their source. Christ suffered temptations but gave no heed to them.

Satan seeks to deceive and corrupt and, overall, is quite successful. The scriptures inform us that he deceives the whole world (see Revelation 12:9). He is skillful at imitation and tries to make evil appear good and good evil. When possible, he will present himself as an angel of light, or even as the Only Begotten (see Moses 1:19). Lacking real substance, he is all about appearances. When the Lord establishes a church, Satan seeks to corrupt it. The Lord has the priesthood. Satan sets up his own imitation priesthoods and seeks to entice those in the Lord's priesthood to misuse theirs. His purpose is to lead us away from God and to destruction.

When Joseph entered the Sacred Grove to pray, he first encountered dark forces before the pillar of light. Moses, after he met the Lord, also encountered Satan (Moses 1:2, 12). In his vision, Lehi wandered in a dark waste for many hours before calling upon God for mercy and finding the light. In our journey back to God, we will encounter both influences. The temple warns us of Satan's teachings and influence here in our lives and in the world around us.

The same thing occurred in the early days of the Restoration in Kirtland. The spiritual manifestations there included both true and false ones. It required the Holy Ghost and sometimes revelation to discern. In part, we can discern by the content of the message. "That which doth not edify is not of God, and is darkness" (D&C 50:23). True spirits will testify of and point to Christ and lead us to repentance. They edify, enlighten, and are clear. Mormon gives us the key to judging: "Every thing which inviteth to do good, and to persuade to believe in Christ, is sent forth by the power and gift of Christ" (Moroni 7:16).

On the other hand, false spirits deny Christ and encourage us to be lifted up in pride. These influences whisper that we are better than others and appeal to our vanity. They often contradict the scriptures and appeal to our carnal natures. They may spread confusion and darkness. False spirits encourage self-aggrandizement over service and sacrifice. Or, as Mormon concluded, "Whatsoever thing persuadeth men to do evil, and believe not in Christ, and deny him, and serve not God, then ye may know with a perfect knowledge it is of the devil; for after this manner doth the devil work, for he persuadeth no man to do good, no, not one; neither do his angels; neither do they who subject themselves unto him" (Moroni 7:17).

Korihor testified that the devil deceived him by appearing in the form of an angel (see Alma 30:53). He should have avoided the deception by recognizing the message was not authentic because it contradicted existing scripture. But because the instructions were "pleasing unto the carnal mind," Korihor wanted to believe. Rather than ask God for further clarity, he chose to accept the devil's words. They presented an easier path and were popular and accepted by others. Korihor became lifted up in pride and popularity as he taught these things. His success led him to the conviction that what he was teaching must be true. And so he went about deceiving others until God, through Alma, cursed him.

We must avoid making a similar mistake, both in accepting and in teaching false doctrines. "And now, my brethren, seeing that ye know the light by which ye may judge . . . see that ye do not judge wrongfully" (Moroni 7:18).

Homework

1. Learn to better listen to the voice of the Spirit. Ask the Lord to help you recognize His answers. Don't confuse what you might want with what the Lord tells you. Many times, I felt pretty certain about something, but after asking I received totally different instructions from the Lord. Seek to know His will, and then go do it even if it takes a few steps of faith into the dark.

2. Keep a record of the things the Lord tells you. I keep a separate journal of these things. I call it *My Spiritual Journey*. It is not

intended to share with anyone else. It is a record of my questions and answers and the revelations and the experiences I've received from the Lord. It contains our conversations. Sometimes, I record thoughts or insights from my scripture study. It has become like my own personal Doctrine and Covenants. Not only does it preserve these things; it also helps me see my overall progress as I look back through it.

3.   Have absolute faith in the word of God to you. When you, like Nephi, receive direct personal promises from God, you can have absolute faith in those outcomes. God's promises may be given unconditionally, or conditioned upon your doing something. But if you meet the conditions, He always performs. Jacob testi-fied that our existence and the earth upon which we stand came about by the power of God's word (see Jacob 4:9). So when God speaks to you, you can have absolute faith in His word, as surely as you live and as surely as the earth is beneath your feet.

As you do these things, you will grow to reach the point where the Lord can and will give you personal, detailed, and even lengthy revelations, like those in the Doctrine and Covenants. I promise He wants to talk with you. Learn to ask and to listen.

4.   Study "The Candle of the Lord" by Elder Boyd K. Packer (*Ensign*, January 1983). This is a great talk on learning to better recognize the voice of the Spirit. If you are not receiving revelation regularly, how could you change that?

5.   Study "Cast Not Away Therefore Your Confidence" by Elder Jeffrey R. Holland (Ensign, March 2000).

6.   Study "Cleansing the Inner Vessel" (*Ensign*, April 1986) and "Beware of Pride" (*Ensign*, April 1989), both by President Ezra Taft Benson. Pride is one of the challenges we face as Latter-day Saints and, ironically, can creep into our lives as a result of our ordinances and perceived "worthiness."

CHAPTER 7

Conclusion

"Thus saith the Lord of hosts; Consider your ways."

—Haggai 1:7

One of my favorite stories from the Old Testament is found in the book of Haggai. Following the departure of Lehi and his family, the Babylonians under King Nebuchadnezzar destroyed Jerusalem and the temple of Solomon. Many Jews were carried away captive back to Babylon, some were scattered, and few remained behind. This surviving remnant eventually intermarried with the Assyrians and other peoples, and their posterity became the biblical Samaritans.

About fifty years later, King Cyrus of the Persians conquered Babylon and appointed Darius as king. Under his rule, permission was granted for Zerubbabel and Joshua the Priest to lead a group of Jews back to Jerusalem to rebuild their temple. These Jews arrived to find much of the city still in ruins. The surrounding lands had been neglected for half a century, and food was scarce. Despite these challenges, work soon commenced on the foundation of the temple. The altar of sacrifice was restored and worship resumed. The Samaritan Jews who had remained behind offered to help. However, this offer was spurned, and these Samaritans then opposed and hindered the project. Gradually, the initial enthusiasm faded, and the work sat largely neglected while the Jews turned their full attention to survival.

Sixteen years passed with little, if any, work completed on the temple. It was at this point that the prophet Haggai entered the scene with a message from the Lord: "Thus saith the Lord of hosts; consider your ways" (Haggai 1:7). These Jews had neglected their purpose, and as a result, the Lord had hedged up their way.

Haggai reminded the people that they had sown much and reaped little. They were working for wages, only to put them into a "bag with holes" (Haggai 1:6). Their problem was in seeking their own prosperity while the Lord's house lay in ruins. Fortunately, these Jews heeded Haggai's message and repented. Work recommenced immediately upon the temple. Four years later, it was completed.

Still, Haggai's question remains. It is perhaps a good one for each of us. Do we need to consider our ways? Do we neglect the Lord's house because we are too wrapped up in the pursuit of our daily labors? Do our covenants play a central role in our lives? Is our attendance at church and the temple changing our daily walk, or do we attend simply out of a sense of duty?

It is easy to scoff at the Zoramites with their Rameumpton. But then sometimes we make the same error by attending the temple (perhaps smugly, feeling better than others by so doing) and then not thinking of it again until we return. We need to learn at the temple, implement what we learn in our daily lives, and return to the temple again and again. Or, as my stake president likes to say, "We need to get us in the temple, and the temple in us."

Our Temple Journey

Once we have worthily received the ordinances of the temple for ourselves, what more do we need to do? What more does the Lord intend for us to learn? I hope this book has helped you seek answers to these questions.[104]

In the Book of Mormon, we find two responses to the law of Moses and its ordinances. After arriving in the New World, Nephi built a temple like the temple of Solomon (see 2 Nephi 5:16). He taught his people to observe and keep all of the law of Moses, along with its rites and ordinances (see 2 Nephi 5:10). Undoubtedly, he also taught them the meaning or purpose behind the law and ordinances. His brother Jacob explained, "For this intent we keep the law of Moses, it pointing our souls to him [Christ]; and for this cause it is sanctified unto us for righteousness" (Jacob 4:5). These Nephite priests taught the law of Moses and the purpose behind it (see Jarom 1:11). They understood the law and the ordinances as a means to bring them unto Christ. They also saw it as a testimony of Him and His atoning sacrifice (see Alma 34:14).

Likewise, the Lamanite converts of Ammon and his brethren also kept the law of Moses but looked forward to Christ's coming. They understood that the law of Moses was intended to teach them about Christ. "Now they did not suppose that salvation came by the law of Moses; but the law of Moses did serve to strengthen their faith in Christ" (Alma 25:16).

On the other hand, we find others who also taught and practiced the law of Moses but missed the purpose behind it. Some mistakenly believed that salvation came by the law. For example, Sherem confronted Jacob and accused him of perverting and changing the law of Moses into the worship of a being who would come hundreds of years in the future, namely Christ (see Jacob 7:7). Sherem taught that the law of Moses was the *right way*, or that salvation came through the law. He denied Christ. His view of the law of Moses was exactly opposite of Jacob's. And Sherem wasn't alone in his belief. The wicked priests of Noah also taught that salvation came by the law of Moses (see Mosiah 13:27). They made the law of Moses an end in itself and failed to see that it was nothing without Christ.

I used to believe that qualifying for and worthily receiving the temple's ordinances was all that was necessary. After that, you just had to *endure* to the end and you'd be saved. I saw the challenge of this life as becoming and then staying worthy of a temple recommend. Then the endowment would somehow provide us with our *recommend* for the next life. Or, in other words, I thought salvation came through the ordinances, just as Sherem believed people would be saved by obedience to the law of Moses.

Today, I view the temple ordinances as necessary but as the means to greater ends, one of which is to prepare us to return into Christ's presence. Like the law of Moses, our ordinances contain types and shadows of these underlying realities. We need to receive these realities, not just the ceremonial depictions of them contained in the ordinances. It is not enough to simply enact the return to Christ's presence through ceremony; we must make the actual journey.

The ordinances extend an authorized invitation.[105] While the invitation may be necessary, it is not the full blessing. There is another step involved. We must press on and meet the conditions to see the eventual realization of the promised blessings. This pattern should not be surprising because we encounter it over and over in the gospel. For example, after baptism, we are confirmed by the laying on of hands and are commanded to receive the Holy Ghost. This is our invitation and admonition to receive it in the ordinance. The actual baptism of fire of the Holy Ghost follows our offering up the sacrifice of a broken heart and contrite spirit (3 Nephi 9:20).

Likewise, we may be ordained to the priesthood and given authority. Receiving power in that priesthood is another matter. It depends upon righteous living and the Spirit of the Lord (see D&C 121:36–41). These blessings don't always follow automatically. More is required of us after the initial invitation. Unfortunately, some receive the invitation and fail to press on to find the promised blessing. Hence we are warned that many are called, but few are chosen (see D&C 121:34). Both steps are necessary, but recognize that they are two entirely different things. We must be called and we must also be chosen. Do not be content with the first and fail to receive the second.

It is the same in the temple. The temple initiatory, endowment, and sealing ordinances extend authorized blessings and invitations to us. These blessings are given conditionally, based upon our subsequent faithfulness. The ceremonies point toward much greater blessings. Press on until you receive them. These blessings include baptism by fire and the Holy Ghost, having your calling and election made sure, and receiving the Second Comforter. If we have eyes to see, the temple testifies of these things. It is no wonder then that, in one of his final addresses to the Saints, Joseph exclaimed, "Oh! I beseech you to *go forward, go forward and make your calling and your election sure;* and if any man preach any other Gospel than that which I have preached, he shall be cursed."[106]

The mistakes some of the ancient Israelites made should give us pause in our own journey. Let us learn from them and not repeat their errors. Their mistakes included rejecting blessings the Lord and Moses wanted them to receive (see D&C 84:23–24); failing to see and understand the underlying testimony and purpose behind their ordinances; being lifted up in pride because of their status as a covenant people, thereby distancing themselves from God and turning these blessings into condemnation; and missing the gospel principles of charity, love, service, repentance, and sacrifice for others and focusing instead on outward appearances and adding their own rules, traditions, and customs to the Lord's commandments (like counting steps on the Sabbath day). The result of these mistakes was that many of them rejected the Messiah who gave them their ordinances and commandments when He walked and lived among them.

As Latter-day Saints, we can be prone to the same problems. Do we reject the Lord's blessings by failing to believe the promises contained in the scriptures? Or do we believe them but think they apply to others, or to some great prophet but not to us? Can we see and understand the purposes for our ordinances? If not, are we asking for further light and knowledge from the Lord? Do we allow these things to lift us up in pride? Does our knowledge of the gospel cause us to seek to serve and lift others, or do we feel smugly superior as we go about our lives, failing to recognize our increased accountability? Are we repenting, receiving the mighty change of heart, and seeking for charity toward others? Or are we judging others and worrying about whether our neighbor is drinking a caffeinated soda? We must learn from the mistakes of ancient Israel or be doomed to repeat the past.

Coming unto Christ

The temple endowment invites each of us, individually and personally, to come unto Christ. It provides us with keys that can unlock the powers of godliness in our individual lives. One of the most practical ways to grow closer to our Savior is to go to Him in prayer and ask Him what you still lack. There is probably a whole list, so just ask for one thing. What's next? Listen for His answer, and then go do whatever He tells you to do. When you have accomplished the task He required, return and report back to Him. You will then learn more and receive further instructions. Repeat this process over and over. You will find your heart changing and your feet on a path returning you to Him.

Doctrine and Covenants 93 was given so that we might know whom we worship and how to worship Him (see D&C 93:19). The first verse of that section contains a formula that perhaps best summarizes one of the purposes of our endowment. It reads, "Verily, thus saith the Lord: It shall come to pass that every soul who forsaketh his sins and cometh unto me, and calleth on my name, and obeyeth my voice, and keepeth my commandments, shall see my face and know that I am" (D&C 93:1). In closing, let's consider this promise carefully.

Verily, thus saith the Lord. That should grab our attention. What follows is something we can absolutely rely upon. God's word cannot be unfulfilled (see Isaiah 55:11). His word becomes the law upon which all things operate. What follows is something we can have absolute faith in because it is the word of God.

Every soul. This includes everyone, both young and old, male and female. It includes you and me. No one is excluded. What follows is not limited to prophets, Apostles, leaders, men, women, or any other subcategory. It is open to all. All are alike unto God, who is no respecter of persons.

Who forsaketh his sins. In our youth, we often see this backward. We sometimes view the commandments as restrictive. In reality, it is our sins that hold us back. Forsake them.

And cometh unto me. We forsake our sins by coming unto Christ. There is a spark of Deity in each of us that longs for home. The longing we sense is the absence of the presence of God, or a yearning for our true home. Christ descended to make our return possible. We come unto Him through the laws and ordinances of His gospel. The path to Him is the doctrine of Christ.[107]

And calleth on my name. Prayer is essential. Individually, we each must connect with heaven. We are given the Holy Ghost as a guide. Take your questions to the Lord and let Him teach and lead you. Learn to receive and recognize revelation in your life. "Salvation cannot come without revelation."[108] Recognize His voice and how He speaks to you. Remember the promise, "If thou shalt ask, thou shalt receive revelation upon revelation, knowledge upon knowledge, that thou mayest know the mysteries and peaceable things—that which bringeth joy, that which bringeth life eternal" (D&C 42:61).

And obeyeth my voice. God responds to our earnest prayers. We will be given direction. We then need to follow it by acting upon the answers we've received. As we do so, our belief becomes faith, especially when the answer we act upon isn't one we wanted to hear. Do it anyway. A confirmation you are doing God's will follows acting in faith.

And keepeth my commandments. God's commandments are given to protect, lift, and bless us. He knows how to best adapt them to our individual circumstances. Obedience is also key to receiving further light and knowledge. We receive light and truth by keeping the commandments, and we lose it through disobedience (see D&C 93:28, 39). Our understanding is meant to grow from the early shades of dawn until we eventually stand in the light of the noonday sun. We are meant to qualify ourselves to learn and understand the mysteries of God.

Shall see my face and know that I am. This is one purpose of the temple and the gospel. It is ultimately about your redemption from the Fall and bringing you back into the Savior's presence so He can prepare you to return to the Father. "The way for man is narrow, but it lieth in a straight course before him, and the keeper of the gate is the Holy One of Israel; and he employeth no servant there; and there is none other way save it be by the gate" (2 Nephi 9:41). Those in scripture who received this blessing during mortality invite us to do the same. Moses stood in the Lord's presence. He then sought diligently to prepare his people for the same blessing (see D&C 84:23–24). Nephi, Jacob, and Moroni did as well (see 1 Nephi 6:4; Jacob 1:7; Ether 12:41). So did Joseph Smith. Virtually all who have received this blessing invite us to come, see, and do likewise.

Religion isn't just a set of moral guidelines and rules, important as they may be. Nor is it merely congregational worship, meetings, and sets of ordinances, important as those may be. At the heart of it all is our own experience with God. It is coming to know Him, experiencing the mighty change of heart, and becoming like Him. It is deeply personal and individual. Eternal life is knowing Him (see John 17:3). The Savior Himself testified, "Behold, I stand at the door, and knock: if any man [or woman] hear my voice, and open the door, I will come in to him, and will sup with him, and he with me" (Revelation 3:20). He really means it. He is knocking at the door of your life.

May we each open up to Him, I pray, in His Holy Name, Amen.

Endnotes

1. David O. McKay, "David O. McKay Temple Address," an address on the temple ceremony given on September 25, 1941, at the Salt Lake Temple Annex, Utah (manuscript in BYU Library Collections). A copy of the text is available at my website, www.understandingyourendowment.com. President McKay's talk is well worth reading.

2. Ezra Taft Benson, "What I Hope You Will Teach Your Children about the Temple," *Ensign*, August 1985.

3. Why do we not speak more openly about temple ordinances? I believe there are several important reasons for this. One is context. We should respect the Lord's desire that ordinances be given in the temple, a sacred place consecrated and dedicated for that purpose (see D&C 124:37–42). Taking these things out of the temple risks removing them from their proper context. Even the physical place within the temple where various ordinances take place is significant. Change or remove the context, and we risk changing the meaning. We are all familiar with how meanings can change when statements are taken out of context. Another reason is the audience and their preparation to receive these things. We do not wish to cast pearls before swine, so to speak. There are items in this book that may be entirely appropriate for a temple preparation class but not for a general family audience in a sacrament meeting. As indicated in

the preface, this book is written for believing, active members of the LDS faith who have already been endowed. If that isn't you, you may reconsider whether this will have value, or even make sense to you. Yet another reason for not speaking more openly may be that many who are willing to talk about the temple teach things they don't understand and are often incorrect. Your endowment should be between you and the Lord. You should rely primarily upon Him to teach you through the Spirit. He will teach us as we prepare to receive more. All of that said, we should also recognize that in appropriate times and places and audiences, we can and perhaps should say more. The covenants we make in the temple are that we won't disclose certain names, signs, and tokens. Sometimes we extend that prohibition to cover every aspect of the temple and therefore say nothing at all, with the result that many members understand little about the temple. There are many aspects of temple service that we can and should discuss. I have prayerfully and carefully tried to seek an appropriate balance in this book. Some may think it says too much, and others perhaps not enough.

4.   H. Clay Trumbull, *The Blood Covenant: A Primitive Rite and Its Bearings on Scripture* (Kirkwood, Missouri: Impact Christian Books, 1975). In 1885, Professor Trumbull, a theologian, gave a series of lectures, presenting his research into primitive rites of covenanting among biblical and non-biblical peoples. Of particular interest to Dr. Trumbull was the practice of blood covenants. His work was eventually published. The covenant practices and many of the ideas outlined in this chapter are contained in his work. I am indebted to a friend, Jack Kelley, for bringing the covenant steps and Dr. Trumbull's work to my attention.

5.   See James L. Garlow, *The Covenant: a Study of God's Extraordinary Love for You* (Kansas City: Beacon Hill Press, 2007), 22–26. Dr. Garlow's work presents much of Dr. Trumbull's work in a more accessible manner. For example, Dr. Garlow's book clearly identifies the various steps in covenant ceremonies. These steps are contained in Dr. Trumbull's original work, but are not as clearly ordered and spelled out.

6.   See JST Genesis 9:15, 21–25; 14:27; Genesis 15; 17:10–14; 26:3–5; 28:13–15.

7.   See Trumbull, *The Blood Covenant*, 12–96.

8.   See, for example, 2 Samuel 13:18, where Tamar's robe indicated her status as royalty and a virgin.

9.   This exchange may have been Jonathan's acceptance and recognition that God had anointed David to be the next king of Israel through Samuel—if Jonathan was aware of that fact at the time. See 1 Samuel 16:1–14.

10. We find another example of this in Genesis 14:13, where Mamre, Eschol, and Aner were in covenant with Abram. Abram later called upon these three to help him battle to free his nephew Lot when Lot was captured (Genesis 14:24). See Trumbull, *The Blood Covenant*, 265.

11. It is possible that Goliath understood exactly what he was doing. He may have believed that he had the favor of whatever pagan deity he worshipped and may have intentionally defied Israel's God.

12. D&C 109:24–28. Isaiah expressed a similar idea (see Isaiah 54:17), which the Savior repeated to the Nephites: "No weapon that is formed against thee shall prosper; and every tongue that shall revile against thee in judgment thou shalt condemn. This is the heritage of the servants of the Lord, and their righteousness is of me, saith the Lord." (See 3 Nephi 22:17; see 11–17); also 2 Nephi 6:17: "For the Mighty God shall deliver his covenant people. For thus saith the Lord: I will contend with them that contendeth with thee."

13. Dr. Trumbull traced this rite through Egypt, Canaan, and other ancient Semitic races, but also pointed out that it is found in Africa, Europe, China, India, and among Polynesian and Native American races. He stated, "Proofs of the existence of this rite of blood-covenanting have been found among primitive peoples of all quarters of the globe; and its antiquity is carried back to a date long prior to the days of Abraham" (Trumbull, *The Blood Covenant*, 206).

14. Trumbull, *The Blood Covenant*, 4–6.

15. See Ibid., 9.

16. Ibid., 203. It is also interesting to note that, in some cases, these covenants were performed by proxy (Trumbull, 26–27).

17. Ibid., 6.

18. Arabic cultures have the same idea, but they say that blood is thicker than milk. Children nourished by the same mother are referred to as "milk brothers" or "suckling brothers." Blood brothers are bound closer than "milk brothers." See Ibid., 10–11.

19. Ibid., 264.

20. In addition to covenant, another meaning of *be'rith* is a bond, or a joining together, deriving from the Akkadian root *biritu*, meaning to fetter or chain. So to "cut" a covenant is to bind or chain oneself in an absolute, binding compact. The covenantal meal or feast is also referenced in the Hebrew word *be'rith*, which, in addition to something cut, can signify something eaten. See Victor Ludow, "Covenants."

21. Joseph Smith taught, "Man was not able himself to erect a system, or plan with power sufficient to free him from [the] destruction which awaited him. . . . [Therefore] God prepared a sacrifice in the gift of His own Son . . . to open a door through which man might enter into the Lord's presence, whence he had been cast out for disobedience. . . . By faith in this atonement or plan of redemption, Abel offered to God a sacrifice that was accepted, which was the firstlings of the flock. Cain offered of the fruit of the ground, and was not accepted, because he could not do it in faith . . . he could not exercise faith contrary to the plan of heaven. It must be shedding the blood of the Only Begotten to atone for man; for this was the plan of redemption; and without the shedding of blood there was no remission [of sins]; and as the sacrifice was instituted for a type, by which man was to discern the great Sacrifice which God had prepared; to offer a sacrifice contrary to that, no faith could be exercised, because redemption was not purchased in that way . . . consequently Cain could have no faith; and whatsoever is not of faith, is sin. But Abel offered an acceptable sacrifice, by which he obtained witness that he was righteous" (Joseph Smith, *Teachings of the Prophet Joseph Smith* [Salt Lake City: Deseret Book, 1977], 58–59).

22. For further explanation of why Abel's sacrifice was acceptable and Cain's was not, see *Teachings of the Prophet Joseph Smith*, 58.

23. Trumbull, *The Blood Covenant*, 211; emphasis added.

24. The Apostle Paul clearly understood and taught the concept of our becoming one with the Savior. See, for examples, 1 Corinthians 6:15–20; Ephesians 5:30; and the Savior's prayer in 3 Nephi 19:23.

25. See Trumbull, *The Blood Covenant*, 238–40.

26. See H. Clay Trumbull, "The Ten Commandments as a Covenant of Love," *The Salt Covenant* (Kirkwood, Missouri: Impact Christian Books, 2000) for a more detailed discussion of the Ten Commandments as covenant terms and conditions.

27. Obviously, the Doctrine and Covenants also contain important covenant teachings such as the oath and covenant of the priesthood, the law of consecration, and the new and everlasting covenant of marriage, among many others (see D&C 42; 84; 132, and so on). The Pearl of Great Price likewise adds important clarifications to the Abrahamic covenant (Abraham 2:7–12). The Book of Mormon has been referred to by the Lord as the new covenant (D&C 84:55, 57). One of its primary purposes, as stated on the title page, is to make known "the covenants of the Lord."

From the Bible were taken many plain and precious truths of the gospel and many covenants of the Lord (1 Nephi 13:26). The result is an "awful state of blindness" (1 Nephi 13:32). The Book of Mormon restores these lost truths and covenants (1 Nephi 13:35–36) and contains the fulness of the gospel (Joseph Smith—History 1:34).

28. JST version cited.

29. In fact, verse 6 points to Abraham's great faith in the Lord's promise of a yet unborn heir. The Joseph Smith Translation confirms this.

30. The biblical text does not say whether Abraham was specifically commanded to do this by the Lord, or if he was already familiar with it and knew what was coming because of local practice—in which case, he didn't need to be told what to do.

31. The blood-path rite was also found in arranging marriages in Middle Eastern desert communities. The father of the groom, as the greater of the two parties, would walk barefoot between the animal parts, promising that his son would be a good husband. He would be followed by the father of the bride, walking the same path and promising that his daughter was a virgin and would be a good wife. The walk through the blood-path represented the penalty if either party proved false to these promises.

32. Jeremiah 34:18, 20. This imagery also gives added meaning to scriptures mentioning being cut or divided asunder (for example, Hebrews 4:12; Matthew 24:51). Also, in the well-known story of Ruth and her mother-in-law, in Ruth's response there is an interesting phrase: "the Lord do so to me [presumably Ruth made a gesture at this point], and more also, if ought but death part thee and me" (Ruth 1:17).

33. These events of Abraham's life are so sparsely recorded in the Bible, it seems safe to assume that this verse has something of significance and is not merely a passing comment. Biblical scholars have surmised that the root Hebrew *ayit*—here "birds of prey"—is likely the carrion-eating falcon. In Egyptian art, this bird represents the god Horus, with whom the Pharaoh was identified. It may be that these fowls symbolically foreshadowed the captivity of Abram's future posterity at the hands of the Egyptians and their subsequent return through the merits of the patriarch and his covenant from the Lord. This interpretation seems to be confirmed by the prophecy contained in verses 13–16.

34. For example, in the New Testament, the story of Ananias and Sapphira, who lied to the Lord and lost their lives, may seem harsh unless one

realizes that they were under covenant to live the law of consecration and had reached a level where they were fully accountable. So by their deception, they deliberately broke their covenant, thereby incurring the penalty (see Acts 5:1–10). Understanding covenant penalties and the seriousness of covenants sheds further light on an incident from the life of Moses. After being in the Lord's presence and receiving the assignment to free the Israelites, as Moses was returning to Egypt, "the Lord met him, and sought to kill him" (Exodus 4:24). What had Moses done to so anger the Lord? He had failed to circumcise his eldest son. Not by deliberate action, but through neglect, Moses had jeopardized the covenant (see Genesis 17:14). Immediately, Zipporah, his wife, took a sharp stone and corrected the problem. She stated, "Surely a bloody husband [one newly bound through blood] art thou to me" (Exodus 4:25). As a result, the Lord let Moses go. Zipporah then stated, "A bloody husband thou art, because of the circumcision" (Exodus 4:26). The Hebrew word *khathan*, here translated "husband," denotes a binding through severing or a covenant by blood. Both ideas are found in the marriage rite and in the rite of circumcision. By her statement, "it is as though Zipporah had said: 'we are now newly covenanted to each other, and to God, by blood; whereas, but for this, we should have been [condemned] to slaughter or death" (Trumbull, *The Blood Covenant*, 222–23).

35. See Bruce H. Porter and Stephen D. Ricks, "Names in Antiquity: Old, New, and Hidden" *By Study and Also by Faith*, ed. John M. Lundquist and Stephen D. Ricks (Salt Lake City: Deseret Book and FARMS, 1990), for a more detailed discussion of the importance of names.

36. Ibid.

37. Ibid.

38. Garlow, *The Covenant*, 25.

39. Ibid., 24.

40. Trumbull, *The Blood Covenant*, 65.

41. Marks have also been used to identify groups who have been separated. The Lord set a mark upon Cain, for example. Was this, in part, a mark indicating his covenant with Satan? The Lord cursed the Lamanites and, as a token of this curse, set a mark upon them to keep them separate from His people (Alma 3:6–10). The Amlicites, likewise, marked themselves with red upon their foreheads to set themselves apart (Alma 3:13–18). And, in the final scenes, those who follow Satan will also receive his mark upon their foreheads or in their hands (Revelations 20:4).

42. Perversions of this idea led to cannibalism in some cases. Among some North American Indian tribes (the Huron, Iroquois, and Dakotas, for example), a common practice was to eat the heart of a defeated enemy, in the belief that the warrior doing so would receive the strength and courage of his foe, added to his own (Trumbull, *The Blood Covenant*, 128). There may have been something akin to this in the winding-up scenes of the Book of Mormon, when the Nephites in Moriantum engaged in cannibalism (see Moroni 9:10).

43. See H. Clay Trumbull, *The Threshold Covenant* (Kirkwood, Missouri: Impact Christian Books, 2000), for an enlightening discussion on the sacred importance and symbolism of the threshold and doorposts, the sacrifices related to them, how the smearing of the blood was a welcome to Jehovah, and how the event was symbolic of Christ as the bridegroom and Israel as His bride.

44. Obviously trees and rocks are not the only two physical items employed as covenantal witnesses. Another notable item is the ark of the covenant. John the Revelator saw its final resting place in the temple in heaven (see Revelation 11:19).

45. In addition, Moroni 7:31 teaches us that the work of angels is to fulfill the covenants of the Father.

46. See John W. Welch, *The Sermon at the Temple and the Sermon on the Mount* (Salt Lake City: Desert Book, 1990). Chapter three contains an enlightening analysis of the Savior's sermon as a temple text.

47. Joseph Fielding Smith ed., *Teachings of the Prophet Joseph Smith* (Salt Lake City: Deseret Book, 1977), 162.

48. The term *ordinance* can also be used to refer to a law or an authoritative decree, but for our purposes in this chapter, *ordinance* refers to a religious rite or ceremony.

49. *Teachings of the Prophet Joseph Smith*, 331.

50. Ibid., 309; emphasis added.

51. There are many reasons the Lord uses symbolism, in addition to the ones discussed in the text. They might include the following: symbols encourage us to have a prayerful, searching attitude; symbols understood can impact our minds and leave a longer, more lasting impression than words alone; symbols protect what is sacred and prevent us from being accountable for truths before we are prepared to receive them (see Matthew 13:10–13; many symbols are timeless and universal and can bridge differences in

culture, language, nationality, age, and so on more easily than language; symbols can be really personal, so your understanding of a symbol may be different from mine, and both may be correct. You may see other reasons as well.

52. John A. Widtsoe, "Temple Worship," *Utah Genealogical and Historical Magazine*, April 1921, 62; cited in David B. Haight, "Come to the House of the Lord," *Ensign*, April 1992.

53. See John Welch, *Chart 92: A Comparison of Lehi's Dream and Nephi's Vision* (FARMS), available online (https://byustudies.byu.edu/book_of_mormon_charts/charts/92.pdf).

54. For one reference on gospel symbols, see Alonzo L. Gaskill, *The Lost Language of Symbolism: An Essential Guide for Recognizing and Interpreting Symbols of the Gospel* (Salt Lake City: Deseret Book, 2003). Gaskill's book may be a helpful resource and contains some wonderful insights, though his interpretations are by no means comprehensive.

55. Silvia H. Allred, "Holy Temples, Sacred Covenants," Ensign, November 2008.

56. David O. McKay, as cited in Truman G. Madsen, *The Temple: Where Heaven Meets Earth* (Salt Lake City: Deseret Book, 2008), 11; emphasis added.

57. *Preparing to Enter the Holy Temple* (Salt Lake City: The Church of Jesus Christ of Latter-day Saints, 2002), 32.

58. Joseph Smith recorded that he was afraid when he first encountered the angel Moroni (see Joseph Smith—History 1:32). Likewise, Isaiah recoiled in fear, stating, "Woe is me! for I am undone; because I am a man of unclean lips . . . for mine eyes have seen the King, the Lord of hosts" (Isaiah 6:5). It was the same with Daniel (see Daniel 10:7–8), with the angel and the shepherds at Christ's birth (see Luke 2:9), and with Peter, James, and John at the Mount of Transfiguration (see Matthew 17:6), among many others.

59. Devery S. Anderson, *The Development of LDS Temple Worship: 1846–2000 A Documentary History* (Salt Lake City: Signature Books, 2011), 99.

60. David O. McKay, *David O. McKay Temple Address*, BYU Library Collections.

61. David O. McKay, cited in Gregory Prince and Wm. Robert Wright, *David O. McKay and the Rise of Modern Mormonism* (Salt Lake City: University of Utah Press, 2005), 277.

62. Ibid.

63. I am indebted to a good friend, Craig Jenkins, for pointing this out to me.

64. Boyd K. Packer, *The Holy Temple* (Salt Lake City: Bookcraft, 1980), 257; emphasis added.

65. Hugh W. Nibley, *Temple and Cosmos* (Salt Lake City: Deseret Book and FARMS, 1992), 64.

66. *Doctrinal History of the Church*, 4:478–79.

67. In two of the older temples of the Church (Salt Lake City and Manti), the endowment ceremony is still performed by ordinance workers as live actors in the drama. Participants move from room to room as the ceremony proceeds and as the initiates progress from one sphere to another. In newer temples, the ceremony is presented through film and continued in an audio presentation. In many of these newer temples, movement from realm to realm (or from one state to another) is simulated by changes in lighting. If you have an opportunity to attend one of the live endowment sessions, it may provide you with a little different perspective. I'm grateful that the Church maintains the Manti and Salt Lake Temples as live endowment sessions.

68. James E. Talmage, *The House of the Lord* (Salt Lake City: Bookcraft, 1962), 99–100.

69. For further development of this idea in the endowment, see Jeremy Oakes, *The Journey: Receiving Our Endowment* (2013), 21–23.

70. See Jeremy Oakes, *The Journey*, 18–19. His idea seems consistent with Joseph Smith's teachings on the signs of the priesthood. "There are certain key words and signs belonging to the Priesthood which must be observed in order to obtain the blessing. The sign of Peter was to repent and be baptized for the remission of sins, with the promise of the gift of the Holy Ghost; and in no other way is the gift of the Holy Ghost obtained" (*Teachings of the Prophet Joseph Smith*, 199).

71. *Teachings of the Prophet Joseph Smith*, 149.

72. Sometimes, the idea of seeking one's calling and election is discouraged. I have had a Church leader tell me that seeking one's calling and election is a selfish notion and should be avoided. Obviously, his counsel was contrary to the scriptures and the teachings of the Prophet Joseph Smith.

73. *Lectures on Faith*, 6:7; emphasis added.

74. Ibid.; emphasis added.

75. Joseph Smith also taught that without this sacrifice, we cannot be saved. "It is vain for persons to fancy to themselves that they are heirs with those, or can be heirs with them, who have offered their all in sacrifice, and by this means obtain faith in God and favor with him so as to obtain eternal life, unless they, in like manner, offer unto him the same sacrifice, and through that offering obtain the knowledge that they are accepted of him" (*Lectures on Faith*, 6:8).

76. *Teachings of the Prophet Joseph Smith*, 306.

77. Ibid., 299.

78. Ibid., 150–51.

79. Bruce R. McConkie, *The Promised Messiah: The First Coming of Christ* (Salt Lake City: Deseret Book, 1978), 582.

80. See 1 Nephi 1:8–15; 2 Nephi 11:3; Enos 1:8, 19 (it is subtle in Enos's record); Ether 3; 12:39; and Mormon 1:15.

81. *Teachings of the Prophet Joseph Smith*, 306.

82. See Denver C. Snuffer Jr., *The Second Comforter: Conversing with the Lord Through the Veil* (Salt Lake City: Mill Creek Press, 2006) for a more detailed discussion of this topic.

83. See Alonzo Gaskill, *The Lost Language of Symbolism*, 78–82.

84. Ibid., chapter 5.

85. See Margaret Barker, *Temple Theology* (London: Society for Promoting Christian Knowledge, 2004), 29.

86. Jeremy Oakes, *The Journey*, 47.

87. See M. Catherine Thomas, "The Brother of Jared at the Veil in Temples of the Ancient Word" (Salt Lake City: Deseret Book and FARMS, 1994).

88. This is more obvious in some of the older temples, where the sealing rooms are part of or immediately adjoin the celestial room. The Manti Utah Temple is a good example. In newer temples, it's not always possible to adjoin the sealing rooms to the celestial room. Nevertheless, they do still function as part of the celestial room.

89. See S. Michael Wilcox, *House of Glory: Finding Personal Meaning in the Temple* (Salt Lake City: Deseret Book, 1995).

90. Visit www.anasazi.org for more information on this organization. See also Arbinger Institute, *The Anatomy of Peace: Resolving the Heart of Conflict* (San Francisco: Berrett-Koehler Publishers, 2008). Many of the principles taught by Anasazi are outlined in this book.

91. Ezra T. Benson, "Beware of Pride," *Ensign*, April 1989.

92. "Covenant Relationships Bear Fruit." From Chad Clark's blog *Seek This Jesus of Whom the Apostles and Prophets Have Written*, entry of October 2013 (http://seekthisjesus.com/2013/10/). Used with permission.

93. Ibid.; emphasis added.

94. *Teachings of the Prophet Joseph Smith*, 324.

95. Ibid., 191.

96. *Lectures on Faith*, 1:11.

97. See "If You Struggle with Fear, You Should Read This," from Danessa Foo's blog Unveiled Wife: Encouraging Wives Daily, posted on October 23, 2014 (http://www.unveiledwife.com/if-you-struggle-with-fear-you-should-read-this/).

98. Jeffrey R. Holland, "Cast Not Away Therefore Your Confidence," *Ensign*, March 2000.

99. For further development of this idea, as found in Nephi's experience with Laban and the brass plates, see Denver C. Snuffer, *The Second Comforter: Conversing with the Lord Through the Veil* (Salt Lake City: Millcreek Press, 2006), 74–78.

100. *Lectures on Faith*, 3:5. This lecture teaches that three things are necessary to exercise faith in God unto salvation. First is the understanding that He exists. Second is a correct understanding of His character and attributes. And third is an actual knowledge that our individual course through life is according to His will.

101. *Teachings of the Prophet Joseph Smith*, 160.

102. *Doctrinal History of the Church of Jesus Christ of Latter-day Saints*, 5:19–21.

103. *Teachings of the Prophet Joseph Smith*, 255–56.

104. Again, I would emphasize that this book is intended to be a beginning. There is so much more to the temple that we cannot discuss here, either because it is too sacred to discuss outside the temple or because those things are simply beyond the scope of what this book is attempting to address. One of the best places to seek further clarification is the scriptures. Andrew Skinner once stated that "all scripture is related to the temple" (Andrew C. Skinner, "Jacob: Keeper of Covenants," *Ensign*, March 1998). I am beginning to see the truth of his words. The scriptures do help us understand the temple ordinances better and vice versa.

105. When Joseph Smith inaugurated the endowment for the first time in this dispensation, he recorded the following: "Wednesday, [May 4, 1842]—I spent the day in the upper part of the store . . . in council with General James Adams, of Springfield, Patriarch Hyrum Smith, Bishops Newel K. Whitney and George Miller, and President Brigham Young and Elders Heber C. Kimball and Willard Richards, instructing them in the principles and order of the Priesthood, attending to washings, anointings, endowments and the *communication of keys* pertaining to the Aaronic Priesthood, and so on to the highest order of the Melchisedek [sic] Priesthood, setting forth the order pertaining to the Ancient of Days, and all those *plans and principles by which any one is enabled to secure the fulness of those blessings* which have been prepared for the Church of the First Born, and come up and abide in the presence of the Eloheim in the eternal worlds. In this council was instituted the ancient order of things for the first time in these last days. And the communications I made to this council were of things spiritual, and to be received only by the spiritual minded: and there was nothing made known to these men but what will be made known to all the Saints of the last days, so soon as they are prepared to receive, and a proper place is prepared to communicate them, even to the weakest of the Saints; therefore let the Saints be diligent in building the Temple, and all houses which they have been, or shall hereafter be, commanded of God to build" (*Doctrinal History of the Church*, 5:1–2; emphasis added).

106. *Teachings of the Prophet Joseph Smith*, 366; emphasis added.

107. The doctrine of Christ is clearly outlined three times in the Book of Mormon. By Nephi in 2 Nephi 31 and 32 and by Christ in 3 Nephi 11 and 27.

108. *Teachings of the Prophet Joseph Smith*, 160.

About the Author

Cory B. Jensen was born and raised in Utah, growing up in the shadow of the Logan Temple. He developed a love for the temple early in life and has been an avid student ever since. He graduated with honors from Brigham Young University with a master's of business administration. A lifelong devoted member of The Church of Jesus Christ of Latter-day Saints, he served a mission in Rome, Italy, and is looking forward to the completion of the temple there.

He and his wife, Traci, are the parents of four children. Together, they currently serve as ordinance workers in the Mount Timpanogos Temple. That service has greatly blessed their lives and marriage, though Cory still hasn't gotten used to getting up at four a.m. for their shift.

He hopes the message of this book will bless your life, enrich your personal temple experience, and help you in your journey to better understanding your endowment.